Pagan Portals

Breath of Spring

How to Survive (and Enjoy)
the Spring Festival

Pagan Portals
Breath of Spring

How to Survive (and Enjoy)
the Spring Festival

Melusine Draco

MOON
BOOKS
Winchester, UK
Washington, USA

JOHN HUNT PUBLISHING

First published by Moon Books, 2023
Moon Books is an imprint of John Hunt Publishing Ltd., No. 3 East Street, Alresford
Hampshire SO24 9EE, UK
office@jhpbooks.net
www.johnhuntpublishing.com
www.moon-books.net

For distributor details and how to order please visit the 'Ordering' section on our website.

ISBN: 978 1 80341 188 0
978 1 80341 189 7 (ebook)
Library of Congress Control Number: 2022942609

A CIP catalogue record for this book is available from the British Library.

Design: Matthew Greenfield

UK: Printed and bound by CPI Group (UK) Ltd, Croydon, CR0 4YY
Printed in North America by CPI GPS partners

We operate a distinctive and ethical publishing philosophy in
all areas of our business, from our global network of authors to
production and worldwide distribution.

Contents

Other Books in the Series

Sumer is Icumen In
ISBN: 978 1 78535 981 1

Harvest Home: In-Gathering
ISBN: 978 1 80341 110 1

Have A Cool Yule
ISBN: 978 1 78535 711 4

Chapter One

Candlemas

When the Romans invaded Britain about 2000 years ago our climate had just about recovered from a cool wet period which had lasted some 2000 years. The Romans enjoyed warm, dry conditions – warm enough to enable them to cultivate grapes successfully at such northerly latitudes. Their departure soon after the year 400CE coincided with a deterioration to cooler, wetter weather that affected the whole of Europe, especially the north. Some centuries later the weather began to improve again and from about 800 to 1300CE, there was a long period of considerable warmth. Winters were mainly wet and mild and summers were warmer than they are today.

The beginning of the 14th-century saw another deterioration in the climate and, by 1350 it had declined so much that our vineyards were no longer viable. The Little Ice Age had arrived and another 500 years were to pass before it relented. This was the period when the Thames and other European rivers often froze during the severe winters, particularly during the 17th and 18th centuries, which were the coldest periods of the Little Ice Age. Yet it was not all a time of unrelieved gloom – the climate often brought hot dry summer spells.

As we can imagine, being possibly the most basic activity in our experience, breathing is also an important magical metaphor. A breath of fresh air is a welcome change from the current situation. This term transfers the idea of fresh air to a new approach or welcome arrival, and has largely replaced both the earlier (mid 1800s) breath of heaven and breath of spring, although the latter is still heard occasionally. Nevertheless, the arrival of spring is eagerly welcomed after the long, dark days of winter and for our superstitious forebears. When Christmas Day was decreed to fall on 25th December, Candlemas was brought forward to 2nd February by the Emperor Justinian in 542CE as a thanksgiving for the ending of a plague. According to 16th century Catholic historian, Caesar Baronius, it was first introduced into Rome by Pope Gelasius c.496 to counteract the pagan *Lupercalia*.

Nevertheless, *Imbolc* is – and was – a pagan holiday celebrated from 1st February until sundown on 2nd February. Based on a Celtic tradition, it was meant to mark the halfway point between Winter Solstice and the Spring Equinox in Neolithic Ireland and Scotland. The holiday is still celebrated by Wiccans and other practitioners of neo-pagan or pagan-influenced religions. *Imbolc* is just one of several pre-Christian holidays highlighting some aspect of the old calendar and sunlight, and heralding the change of seasons dating back to those earlier times in the British Isles.

> Since the Feast of Lights had long been observed on 1st February with a highly developed fire ceremonial in which perambulation with lighted torches, connected with the return of the Goddess from the underworld and the rebirth of nature in the spring, played a prominent part, it is by no means improbable that this ancient festival lay in the background of the Candlemas liturgical rites. Indeed its customs survived in the Christian era long after their original significance had been abandoned and probably forgotten. In Scotland, for example, the sacred fire of Bridget, was carefully guarded and on the Eve of Candlemas a bed made of corn and hay was surrounded with candles as a fertility rite, the fire symbolizing the victorious emergence of the sun from the darkness of winter. [*Seasonal Feasts & Festivals*]

The earliest mentions of *Imbolc* in Irish literature date back to the 10th century. Poetry from that time relates the holiday to ewe's milk, with the implication of purification. It's also been speculated that this stems from the breeding cycle of sheep and the beginning of lactation. The holiday was traditionally aligned with the first day of spring and the idea of rebirth. *Imbolc* celebrations took the form of a festival in honor of the pagan goddess Brigid, who was evoked in fertility rites and oversaw poetry, crafts and prophecy. Brigid was worshipped by the *Filid*, a class of poets and historians among the Celts of ancient Ireland and Britain.

Brigid was considered one of the most powerful Celtic gods, the daughter of the Dagda, the oldest god in the Tuatha du Danann pantheon. She appears in the saga *Cath Maige Tuired* and the *Lebor Gabála Érenn*, a purported history of Ireland collected from various poems and texts in the 10th century. Myths about Brigid's birth say she was born with a flame in her head and drank the milk of a mystical cow from the spirit world. She is also credited with the very first keening, a traditional wailing for the dead practiced at funerals by Irish and Scottish women.

In pre-Christian times, *Imbolc* observance began the night before 1st February and celebrants prepared for a visit from Brigid into their homes by crafting an effigy of the goddess from bundles of oats and rushes. The clothed effigy was placed in a basket overnight and the day was celebrated by burning lamps and lighting bonfires in tribute to her. The goddess Brigid is central to the celebration for modern Wiccans and, in the tradition of the original Celtic festival, Wiccan groups that worship her might include fire rituals on *Imbolc*. Traditions from both the pagan celebration and the Christian observance of St. Brigid's Day can be found in the modern *Imbolc* festivities – while celebrants sometimes make a Brigid's Cross out of reeds, as well as a Brigid corn doll or effigy.

Over the centuries, Brigid was adapted into Christianity

as St. Brigid and accepted as one of Ireland's three patron saints: the Catholic Church claims St. Brigid was a historical person, with accounts of her life written by monks dating back to the 8th century. Brigid (or Bridget) is the patron saint of Irish nuns, newborns, midwives, dairy maids and cattle. In the 12th century, legend held that the nuns in Kildare attended to a fire built in her honour. The fire had burned for 500 years and produced no ash, and only women were allowed in close proximity of the sacred flame. The celebration of St. Brigid's Day on 1st February was put in place by the church to replace *Imbolc* and the festival of the *Cailleach* (a divine hag and ancestor, associated with the creation of the landscape and with the weather, especially storms and winter). On her feast day, an effigy of St. Brigid of Kildare is traditionally washed in the ocean and surrounded by candles to dry, and stalks of wheat are transformed into cross talismans known as 'Brigid crosses'. [*History.com*]

Although Candlemas is a Christian holiday celebrated on 2nd February that has aspects in common with *Imbolc* – it is referred to as Candlemas in accordance with the tradition British Old Craft tradition. Its celebration can be traced to 4th century Greece as a purification holiday and a celebration of the return of light. The modern celebration of *Imbolc* is considered a low-key and sometimes private affair concerned with reconnecting with nature. Since it's a climate-specific holiday, some followers of the Wiccan religion adjust their celebration of it to correspond with a date more appropriate to the coming of spring where they live. Others embrace the symbolism of the holiday and keep to the 1st February celebration.

Since the Victorian era, it is customary to *remove* Yuletide decorations on Twelfth Night ... but up until the 19th century people would keep their decorations up until *Candlemas* Eve.

4

If this custom wasn't followed, it was believed that greenery would not return and vegetation would not grow, leading to agricultural shortages and subsequently food problems. Even though Christmas decorations are now less about foliage and more about baubles, glitter and tinsel, many people still adhere to the superstition which they ascribe to the modern Twelfth Night on the 5th January. This 17th century poem by Robert Herrick gives us a better idea of what sort of greenery was used prior to the introduction of the Victorian Christmas tree ... In his 'Ceremony Upon Candlemas Eve' he wrote ...

DOWN with the rosemary, and so
Down with the bays and mistletoe;
Down with the holly, ivy, all,
Wherewith ye dress'd the Christmas Hall:
That so the superstitious find
No one least branch there left behind:
For look, how many leaves there be
Neglected, there (maids, trust to me)
So many goblins you shall see.

In his longer 'Ceremonies for Candlemas Eve', he added:

DOWN with the rosemary and bays,
Down with the misletoe;
Instead of holly, now up-raise
The greener box (for show).

The holly hitherto did sway;
Let box now domineer
Until the dancing Easter day,
Or Easter's eve appear.

Then youthful box which now hath grace

Your houses to renew;
Grown old, surrender must his place
Unto the crisped yew.

When yew is out, then birch comes in,
And many flowers beside;
Both of a fresh and fragrant kind
To honour Whitsuntide.

Green rushes, then, and sweetest bents (grasses),
With cooler oaken boughs,
Come in for comely ornaments
To re-adorn the house.
Thus times do shift; Each thing his turn does hold;
New things succeed, As former things grow old.

In fact, Herrick (1591-1674) wrote at least four poems concerning Candlemas. Likewise, 'Upon Candlemas Day' shows the day itself had its own entrenched traditions:

END now the white loaf and the pie,
And let all sports with Christmas die.

Finally, in 'The Ceremonies for Candlemas Day', he wrote:

KINDLE the Christmas brand, and then
Till sunset let it burn;
Which quench'd, then lay it up again
Till Christmas next return.
Part must be kept wherewith to tend
The Christmas log next year,
And where 'tis safely kept, the fiend
Can do no mischief there.

This latter poem recalls the tradition that Christmas greenery would be burned and the Yule log allowed to burn down completely, but that a portion should be held back to start next year's Yule log fire (and as a good luck charm against 'mischief'). The ashes were to be spread over the land/garden to ensure a good harvest and the Yule log for the next year would be chosen at that time. Candlemas was also believed to be a good day for weather forecasting (it falls halfway between the Winter Solstice and the Spring Equinox): If it was a sunny day, there would be forty more days of cold and snow. This belief has carried into folklore tradition around the world, and one olde English rhyme says:

If Candlemas Day be fair and bright,
Winter will have another flight;
But if it be dark with clouds and rain,
Winter is gone, and will not come again.

All this Christian overlay merely confirms what an important festival this was for our pagan forebears and, as such, it became the feast of the Purification of the Virgin Mary in the church calendar. The Christian feast-day commemorates the ceremony performed by the mother of Jesus in the temple of Jerusalem forty days after the birth of Christ in fulfillment of the Mosaic Law requiring the cleansing of a woman from the ritual impurity incurred at childbirth. The convenience of having yet another important pagan festival falling within the 'nativity cycle' meant that Brigid easily became a Catholic saint! In the early calendar, on that morning, many candles were lit in the church, symbolically driving out the darkness. In the afternoon, there was feasting all round, with much music as *Candlemas Day* marked the formal end of winter.

In the pagan Celtic world it was *Imbolc*, the festival marking the beginning of spring that has been celebrated since ancient times. It is also a cross quarter day, that midpoint between the Mid-Winter Festival and the Spring Equinox; the name deriving from the Old Irish *imbolg* meaning *'in the belly'*, a time when sheep began to lactate, their udders filled and the grass began to grow. *Imbolc* was a time to celebrate Brigid, as the goddess of inspiration, healing, and smith-craft, with associations to fire, the hearth and poetry. Also called *Là Fhèill Brìghde*, it corresponds to the Welsh *Gŵyl Fair y Canhwyllau* as a traditional festival marking the beginning of spring; it was widely observed throughout Ireland, Scotland and the Isle of Man. Local festivals marking the arrival of the first signs of spring may be named after either the *Cailleach* or Brìghde, while some interpretations have them as the dual face of the same goddess.

Là Fhèill Brìghde, is also the day the *Cailleach* gathers her firewood for the rest of the winter. Legend has it that, if she intends to make the winter last a good while longer, she will make sure the weather on 1st February is bright and sunny, so she can gather plenty of firewood to keep herself warm in the coming months. As a result, people are generally relieved if *Là Fhèill Brìghde* is a day of foul weather, as it means the *Cailleach* is still asleep, will soon run out of firewood, and therefore winter is almost over.

The *Cailleach* is a divine hag, a creatorix, weather and ancestor deity while Brigid is a sort of Celtic Athena, with very similar functions. Although most often presented as a mysteriously veiled, ancient woman, the *Cailleach* is also said to take on the guise of many different beasts and birds as she travels around the rugged landscapes of her homeland. The *Cailleach Béara* is said to be one of the most ancient of mythological beings, appearing as an old crone who brings winter with her blackthorn staff when she appears and who wields incredible power over life and death. Her ability to control the weather and the seasons meant many communities looked upon her with a mixture of reverence and fear.

Candlemas, then, is the re-awakening of the Old Lass within Old Craft belief and also coincides with the Roman *Festa Candelarum*, which commemorated the search for Persephone by her mother Demeter, Persephone having been kidnapped by the King of the Otherworld, Hades. As Persephone was no longer in our world, darkness was everywhere, so her mother used a torch in her search, and in the end obtained a decree that her daughter would be on Earth and Olympus for two thirds of the year (the light period), and in the Other World (Hades) for the other third of the time (winter season). The festival of candles symbolizes the return of the Light.

During medieval times, peasants still carried torches and crossed the fields in procession, praying for purification of the ground before planting. In the early churches, the torches were replaced by blessed candles whose glow was supposed to take away evil; villagers and townsfolk would later take the candles to their houses to bring protection to their homes and family. During the evening, an especially large candle would have been lit while the family gathered around waiting for a celebratory feast, during which plans and promises to be kept through the new season would be discussed and debated until it burned out. It was also customary at sunset to ritually light a candle in each room of the home in honour of the Sun's return. Not surprisingly, in 1543, Thomas Cranmer, Archbishop of Canterbury, banned candles on Candlemas Day because the rites were seen as superstitious, i.e. pagan!

In traditional British Old Craft, however, Old Candlemas/Old Imbolc now falls on the 15th February due to the changes in the calendar. *Imbolc* is mentioned in some of the earliest Irish literature and there is evidence it has been an important date since pre-Christian times: at the Mound of the Hostages on the Hill of Tara the rising sun at *Imbolc* illuminates the inner chamber; the sun also illuminates the chamber at *Samhain*. Our Neolithic ancestors were obviously acutely aware of this time of the year, as were the Celts and the later settlers in the Ireland, each seeming to adopt some of the traditions and beliefs of the previous/existing culture.

In county Meath there are two important Neolithic solar alignments to *Imbolc*. Firstly, on the Hill of Tara, at the Mound of the Hostages a Neolithic passage grave has an entrance directed towards the sunrise on the 8th November and the 4th February, the start and end of winter respectively. As the sun rises it squarely illuminates the back-stone of the chamber for about a week. The stone engravings are illuminated, not by the sun beam directly, but its diffuse reflection from the back stone. Simultaneously in Cairn L on Cairnbane West, Loughcrew, the sun is shining into the monument to perform what can only be described as a carefully choreographed ballet. At the instant of sunrise the first rays of light are focused on a free-standing white pillar stone and nothing else. The light is seen to visibly move from top to bottom in a matter of seconds and then swing from left to right where it is then focused onto a 'mirror' stone which throws the diffuse sunlight into a dark recess illuminating one of the most accomplished pieces of Neolithic art in the world.

This is the only time when the carvings can be seen without the aid of a torch. All the fine detail being revealed in a very dramatic and stunning way. The sunlight then falls on an angled stone and again within a matter of seconds is seen to shrink and disappear as the sun moves higher in the sky outside the chamber. Curiously the central motif on the Mound of the Hostages stone and the Cairn L stone are remarkably similar, sharing images of nested concentric circles. From these ancient rites we can see how they identify with the Old Lass and her awakening, not to mention their association with the Mysteries of the Elder Faith.

In *Witchcraft: A Tradition Renewed*, Evan John Jones acknowledges that Candlemas is the first of the great Sabbats and the start of the ritual year, when it is time to let go of the past and to look to the future, clearing out the old, making both outer and inner space for new beginnings. In ancient Rome, on the eve of Candlemas all the home fires would have been put out, cleaned out, and re-lit being symbolic of the returning light of the Sun. In Old Craft, and in keeping with this symbolism, a broom made from the three sacred woods symbolic of the three-fold aspects of the goddess (the handle from ash, the brush from birch twigs and the binding cord from willow) would be placed by the front door to symbolize sweeping out the old and welcoming in the new.

We are now preparing to move into the bright half of the year and those four great fire festivals that are marked by the Equinoxes and Solstices of the solar year, together with the four traditional celebrations of Old Beltaine, Old Lammas, Old Hallowe'en and Old Candlemas making up the eight Sabbats of the witch's year that will be coming round again. The fire festivals occur at the beginning of each quarter of the solar-tide cycle, with Candlemas marking the end of the reign of the Holly King and heralding the first stirrings of the bright tide of summer of the Primal Goddess.

Add To Your Family Tradition

Although the festival of Candlemas – aside from the church litany – has lost much of its significance, it is not difficult to realise just how significant this time was for our pagan Ancestors. Perhaps it's a good idea to clear out the fire-pit in the garden and take it as an opportunity to burn the Yule greenery with a reciting of one of Herrick's poems as the winter air is perfumed with the fragrance of burning twigs.

And, our Christmas tree is great fuel for an outdoor fire. Cut off the branches to use as kindling, and cut the trunk into logs. Pine is not recommended for burning indoors, as its creosote content makes for sticky, sooty fireplaces but it's perfect for keeping us warm while we're enjoying a Candlemas evening outside. The greenery used to decorate our home for the Christmas season has also served its purpose, and the bonfire from burning them also celebrates the light and warmth of the Old Lass returning to the world on one of the darkest (and often one of the coldest) nights of the year. If we removed our decorations at Twelfth Night, keep them dry in the garage until Candlemas Eve.

Once again, Fire is the most important aspect of this celebration because it symbolizes bringing the light of the Old Lass back to the world and the start of the Old Lad beginning to relinquish his power. Ideally, our inside working space should be flooded with candle-light, and we've found the best method is to place collections of tea-lights in plain glass holders on large glass or silver trays. This gives off the maximum reflection and the trays can be placed safely at different levels in different parts of the rooms.

This is also time to reclaim another pagan tradition that has been absorbed into the church calendar without us realising it. We're given free rein to pile our plates high with thin crêpes or thick pancakes, slathering them with a selection of sweet and savoury spreads and toppings. It's a truly joyous occasion but have you ever stopped, mid-chew, to wonder why we eat pancakes every Spring? Let's bring you up to speed about this religious tradition of and give you the low-own on the true origin of the custom. Nowadays, Pancake Tuesday, more formally known as Shrove Tuesday, falls forty-seven days before Easter. The day is always followed by Ash Wednesday, which is the beginning of Lent, whereby Christians traditionally fast for forty days.

Shrove Tuesday marks the last day before Lent – a period of forty days whereby Christians traditionally fast or give up certain foods. The forty days represent the time that Jesus spent fasting in the desert where he resisted the temptation of Satan. In the past, families would traditionally prepare to fast by using up all the ingredients in their kitchen. These would usually consist of eggs, milk, and flour – everything you need to make a good pancake!

But ... For many people worldwide, a *pagan* Candlemas has a particular smell: not just the scent of lighted candles but also the fragrance of pancakes being cooked for family and friends. Candlemas pancakes should traditionally be made with wheat flour from the previous harvest. Stacks of them can be prepared without fear of famine, since the fields would soon be regaining their golden colour. There was even an old saying that held if you ate pancakes on Candlemas Day, you would be ensured a good harvest in the coming year.

It was also commonly believed that the blessed candle would protect the house from lightning. A superstition concerning the beneficial virtues of this object suggested that a piece of blessed candle placed beneath the threshold of the house would ward off maleficent witchcraft. Candlemas announces the coming of spring and daylight has already increased by one hour. According to a saying: 'Candlemas sun announces spring, flowers and joy'. This day is also important for bee-keepers because it is believed that a clear and limpid sky on Candlemas foretells a beneficial year for bees.

In our Celtic countries, it has always been a tradition to make pancakes at Candlemas. Another saying goes: 'If you want to avoid infected wheat, pancakes at Candlemas do eat'. This custom dates back to the day when new maids and man-servants were hired. To celebrate this and alleviate their sadness about being separated from their family, the mistress of the house took up her frying pan and treated her new staff and the rest of the house to pancakes; a great celebration at the time. This feast was also the opportunity to eat the surplus wheat from an earlier sowing.

When we eat pancakes at Candlemas, all the candles in the house should be lit, which is easy to understand when considering the etymology of the word: in vulgar Latin *festa candelarum* means 'feast of the candles'. Candlemas! Candles that drive back the darkness of winter are lit. Candlemas brings to mind clarity and light. The six dark weeks are past; winter is fading. Candlemas is a prelude of the coming spring to which humans aspire and hope will be a liberation, a new beginning.

The Roman *Candelabrum Festa* was the celebration of *Light* and *Proserpina*, the Goddess of Light was abducted by the God of the Underworld. Proserpina had to spend the six months of autumn and winter alongside her husband as Queen of the Underworld. She spent the remaining months of the year on Earth, helping her mother Demeter, the Goddess of Agriculture and Harvest, to look after spring and summer. During the *Candelarum Festa* Romans lit candles at midnight as a symbol of purification with the candlelight processions that took place on this festival.

Though *la Chandeleur, Fête de la Lumière* or *Jour des crêpes* is often associated with the French Catholic holiday of Candlemas, this also stems from earlier Gallic traditions. While some say *Chandeleur* celebrates the return of sunny days (crêpes symbolize the sun), others say that making crêpes using flour left over from the harvest ensures prosperity in the coming year. The French word for candle is *chandelle* hence *chandeleur* and, while *Chandeleur* is not an official holiday in France, most French also eat pancakes on that day.

There were also some strange practices in France. The first pancake was thrown against a cupboard where it remained for the entire year. If it did not turn mouldy it meant that the house would be guaranteed wealth. Also, holding the frying pan in one hand and a gold sovereign in the other. The true art involves tossing the pancake up in the air and catching it in the frying pan in order to be ensured wealth and abundance. The round shape and its yellowish colour are also an allusion to the coming spring.

There was the tradition of flipping a crêpe while holding a gold coin. The gold coin was then rolled into the crêpe and placed in the master's room on top of a cabinet until the following year.

Peasants also believed that by eating crêpes they were ensuring a healthy wheat harvest for the coming year. The men walked through the fields with torches, while invoking the goddess to purify the land before they started sowing.

- The Church of Rome replaced *Birgit* by *Ste-Brigitte* who is celebrated on 1st February in the calendar of saints.

Some other pagan nations celebrated the Cult of the Bear, when the animal came out of hibernation around *Chandelours – candle bear* celebrated therefore the return of the light in late January, early February. The Church of Rome replaced all these pagan festivals by the *Chandeleur* (candlelight festival or Candlemas Day) during the 5th century, although it had great difficulty in eradicating the Cult of the Bear festival, when bonfires and torch processions were accompanied by mock abductions of girls and fancy-dress parties.

But perhaps you do not know that this day is also linked to old pagan beliefs and that some of them are about bears. In ancient times and in most of the parts of the world where bears were living, this animal was highly feared and respected by humans. The strongest beast known, he could be considered as the king of the forest – and as such, he often had an important place in traditional celebrations and rituals because he is a symbol of strength, power and protection; he is the masculine warrior, king, and protector of the people. *Chandelours – candle bear* celebrated therefore the return of the light late January, early February when the bear also returned to the world.

The bear pagan celebrations were replaced by Christian events, but memories from the ancient beliefs survived down through the centuries. Thus, people have mixed their old cultures and beliefs with the new ones. For example, in France, from the 12th to the 18th century, the 2nd of February was often called, *Chandelours* (*ours* = bear) instead of Chandeleur (the French name for Candlemas). In one word, souvenirs from old pagan cults referring to the light and/or to the bear were surviving through a Christian ceremony. And even today, some villages are still commemorating old traditions and rituals every year in February during bear festivals.

Store-bought crêpes can be warmed in the oven while the celebration is in progress. Set the oven to its lowest temperature and layer the cold crêpes with wax paper between them, then wrap the entire stack in wax paper. Wrap the whole bundle with foil, and leave it in the oven at the lowest setting for one to one and a half hours until thoroughly warmed through. Not as enjoyable as good old-fashioned home-made ones, admittedly, but not as time-consuming, especially if it's a full sabbat-meeting – which it *should* be on this very special night when the Old Lass re-awakens and because this is when we welcome her back.

The floral tributes for Candlemas are those early favourite spring flowers – snowdrops – despite them not being native to the British Isles. They're actually from southern Europe and only came to Britain in the late 16th century, and it took them almost 200 years to become a naturalized wild plant. Seeing snowdrops pop up is one of the first signs that spring is on the way and, since they're supposed to bloom at Candlemas, they're also known as 'Candlemas bells'. But native to our islands or not, who doesn't seek for signs of them in gardens, parks and churchyards on a fine spring day as the first grey-green spears of foliage push through the frosty earth? A small bunch or pot of snowdrops by the door to welcome the guests, perhaps … Or a large vase of the earliest catkins to appear on the hazel trees that can be seen from January through to the spring.

As our first outdoor ritual for the year, this is one of the four fire festivals to mark the turning of the seasons. Each was celebrated for three days – before, during and after the official day of observance. *Imbolc*, which literally means 'in milk', traditionally marked the lactation period of ewes and cows.

Ewes are unable to produce milk until after they bear their young, which occurs at this time. Since milk was very important to the basic survival of the tribes, this was a time of great joy and meant that the end of a long winter was in sight, and green pastures were only a few months away.

During the *Imbolc* ritual it was customary to pour milk (or cream) onto the earth. This was done in thanksgiving, as an offering of nurturing, and to assist in the return of fertility and generosity of the earth to its people (the return of Spring). *Imbolc* was celebrated in honor of Brighid or Brid (pronounced 'Breed'), also known as Brigid, Brigit, or Bride, in her maiden aspect and the daughter of Dagda. *Imbolc* was one of the four great fire festivals, with significance placed upon the Light of fire. At *Imbolc*, Brighid was pregnant with the seed of the Sun. She was ripe with the promise of new life, as the seeds of the earth deep within its soil begin to awaken at this time, ripe with the promise of Spring, new life for the planet. Thus *Imbolc* was a time of awakening, promise and hope for the coming year.

In Mexico and Mexican communities around the globe, the holiday is celebrated with tamales, a traditional Mesoamerican dish, often paired with a warm beverage like atole. On CBC Radio's *All In A Day*, Ottawa's Patricia Ramirez shared her recipe for vanilla-flavoured *atole* – a perfect drink to warm your bones on a cold February day.

Ingredients:

½ cup Maseca corn flour
2 cups water
3 cups milk
1 cinnamon stick
¾ cup of brown sugar or ¼ cup grated piloncillo
(unrefined cane sugar pressed into a cone shape)
1 tbsp. vanilla

Directions:

Add the corn flour to a pot and stir in the water slowly.
Turn the heat to medium-high and add milk.
Add the cinnamon stick and the brown sugar or piloncillo.
Stir for between three to five minutes.
Reduce heat to low and simmer for about five more minutes, stirring often.
Add the vanilla and stir. Remove from heat and serve.

For most pagan households, Candlemas will be a welcome addition to our annual celebrations, so make this your regular date for making and sharing pancakes each year.

Chapter Two

Equinox Turbulence

The Elders of the Coven of the Scales and myself always view the Spring Equinox with a degree of trepidation since it usually brings with it the onset of personal turmoil and upheaval. As the year begins to change, *we* prepare to batten down the hatches until the storm of uncertainty has passed. And, as we all appreciate, uncertainty is often centered on worries about the future and all the bad things we can anticipate happening. It can leave us feeling hopeless and depressed about the days ahead, exaggerate the scope of the problems we face, and even prevent us from taking action to overcome any problems until the Vernal Equinox has gone.

Canadian wellness coach, Kelly Spencer, observes that the Vernal Equinox is a time of rebirth for all life.

As winter places us in a life of more darkness, we rejoice more sunlight. With all of life dependent upon the sun, you can imagine the energy of celebration this time of year for all living species. Birds sing, flowers bloom, bees dance, and babies of all species are born. In ancient times, rituals were performed at the Spring Equinox and people would cleanse old energy. This is where our tradition of 'spring cleaning' came from! We feel more energized and want to plant seeds of vision in our lives or for our gardens. We may feel the urge to open the windows, clean and prepare for a new, warmer and brighter season. We might make plans to get outside more, develop a health plan for ourselves, or set some new goals to achieve, both personally and professionally.

We also understand that there is a real 'seasonal science'

concerning the varied effects on our body and mind so that we can all be more mindful of when transition from season to season wreaks its effects on us. In fact, it can affect all living creatures. Seasonal changes, including the increase in the amount of light is a signal to animals, plants and people, of the changing seasons. For some, changes of season can trigger a change in mood. During the winter many develop seasonal affective disorder (SAD), with some experts believing the shorter days, with less sunlight, upset the body's internal clock causing loss of energy and lack of luster for life.

With the increase in light, as it hits the retina and enters the pineal gland and slows the production of melatonin, we may notice a change in the way we feel and the energy we have. As the melatonin recedes and the light begins to affect the brain, we can get a lighter 'spring' in our step, we become more alert and experience increase feelings of happiness. The fresh air, scents and visual displays of bloom and birth, feel good as we consume them with our senses.

But what can account for those feelings of apprehension that some monumental upheaval is about to occur – and it *will* invariably happen around the Equinox!? There's never been a satisfactory answer to this situation but a gentle read through Professor E O James's *Seasonal Feasts & Festivals* (1961) provided another train of thought.

This related to the tradition custom of seasonal contests that had been an integral element for promoting fertility and conquering the malign forces of evil, especially at the approach of spring. According to Professor James, this is apparent in the many ball games that had survived throughout the ages which originally had a ritual significance – not to mention local hostility. Not infrequently these have occurred in the opening of the year, and have persisted in association with the carnival, revelries and merry-making. The rites, however, belong to the Spring Festival rather than that of the Winter Solstice –

Shrovetide customs looking forward to Easter, not backwards towards Yule.

In England it became the custom for parishes to divide themselves into two opposing groups at this season of the year, which usually coincided with Shove Tuesday, to engage in 'rough and rumbles' such as those recorded in forty-two towns or districts, and in which they have survived to within recent memory. 'Broken shins, broken heads, torn coats and lost hats', we are told were 'among the minor accidents of this fearful contest'. A Frenchman who witnessed the scene remarked that 'if Englishmen called this playing, it would be impossible to say what they would call fighting'.

According to one local tradition this violent event celebrated the driving out and slaying of a cohort of Roman soldiers marching through the town by unarmed Britons. And to suppress the observance in 1846 'it required two troops of Dragoons, a large levy of special constables and the reading of the Riot Act to secure the desired result'. These regional 'needle-matches' or bitterly fought contests between two teams who bear each other a grudge, aroused exceptional personal antagonism between the contestants.

Seasonal games and contests of this nature were almost universal in England and elsewhere in Europe at the approach or beginning of spring, until they were prohibited on the ground that they were dangerous to life and limb, and property, as indeed they were. Is the astral turbulence surrounding the Spring Equinox a throw-back to the 'good old days' enshrined in our racial memory? Because the mere presence of such violence in the astral realm is already acutely burdensome, and to be physically exposed to it is exhausting and debilitating

Uncertain times create waves in the astral realm: When the human mind doesn't know what the future will hold, its natural tendency is to seek out some narrative to grasp on to, to make sense of, and identify with that narrative. Without meditative training, simply remaining in a blank, unknowable present is not how most of us cope with uncertainty. When understood in the context of a society (and, in general, all rules that apply to individuals apply to groups; as above, so below), this means that an uncertain material world (like say, the Corvid pandemic) creates even more uncertainty in our collective heads, and all members of society feel a sense of change, and often of unease, like we know something is coming but aren't sure what. This is what is meant by 'something in the air;' a collective consciousness comes to reflect this uncertainty, this sense of foreboding. It is like the calm before a storm. [*Astral Harmony*]

Both Vernal and Autumnal Equinoxes universally represent a time when earth energies as well as our own bio-energetic systems are dramatically shifting gears, so our emotional and physical health can be quite sensitive, and we need extra rest and care to protect our life force and to help us stay steady.

During equinoxes, the Sun also exerts a stronger pull on the Earth than at the rest of the year, because of the alignment between the sun and the equator. Consequently, the water surface is strongly attracted by the Sun, which accentuates what we call 'great tides'. To the meteorologists, spring is from March to May, and it is seen as a period of instability. This is because the ground is warming up but the air is still quite cold, producing a bitter-sweet mixture of squally showers, fine spells and cold, frosty nights. Just when the days appear to be improving, a deep depression can whip moisture-laden air down from the polar seas, hurling it across the countryside as sleet and snow. After warm March days, when the blackthorn comes into bloom, there is often a sting in the tail of the month – the blackthorn winter!

In fact, the countryman's observation for this time of year is 'Beware the Blackthorn Winter' – because, although the blackthorn is in full bloom by now, its pale, softly fragrant blossoms are often matched by frost-whitened grass or snow-covered hills. The blackthorn flowers before its leaves grow, so we get a real contrast of white flower against black bark; blackthorn has a reputation as being one of the 'witch-trees' of the countryside, not least because we have to be very careful of its long (and very sharp!) spikes which can puncture skin very easily and the wounds have a tendency to turn septic. The blackthorn is depicted in many fairytales throughout Europe as a tree of ill omen but it along with the alder it is the totem tree of traditional British Old Craft.

Called *Straif* in the Ogham, this tree has the most sinister reputation in Celtic tree lore. To witches, it often represents the dark side of the Craft since it is a sacred tree to the Dark, or Crone aspect of the Triple Goddess, and represents the Waning and Dark Moons. Blackthorn is known as the increaser and keeper of dark secrets. The tree is linked with warfare, wounding and death, associated with the *Cailleach* – the Crone of Death, and the Morrigan – since winter begins when the *Cailleach* (in her guise as the goddess of winter) strikes the ground with her blackthorn staff.

The blackthorn's spines are extremely hard and can cause a great deal of bleeding, They were frequently used as pins by English witches and became known as the 'pin of slumber'. The shrub was denounced as a witch's tool by the church and therefore the wood of the blackthorn was often used for the pyres of witches and heretics. Remember where those blossoms are and we also know where to find the sloes to make our sloe gin in the late autumn. Nevertheless, for those who know about these things, the blackthorn is also seen as a protective tree and representative of the endless cycle of life and death. For all its deadly associations the blossoms were used in ancient fertility rites as well as being hung in the bedchamber of a bride on her wedding night.

Witches in northern England would carve the symbol for thorn on a blackthorn staff for protection and the tree itself is also said to be protected by the Faere Folk. Consequently, it is considered a 'fairy tree' and is protected by the *Lunantishee*, a type of fairy that inhabits it. They will not allow a mortal to cut blackthorn on 11th May or 11th November – the original dates of *Beltaine* (May Day) and *Samhain* (All Hallows Eve) according to the Old Calendar. Great misfortune would befall anyone who ignored this advice. [*The Inner-City Path*]

The Spring or Vernal Equinox falls around the 20th-22nd March and is sometimes called the March equinox in the Northern Hemisphere and the September equinox in the Southern Hemisphere. On rare occasions, the equinox can happen just outside of those date ranges to account for leap years. The word equinox is derived from Latin. It means *"equal night."* On the day that the sun passes over the equator, the length of day and night are said to be approximately equal. This means that there will be approximately 12 daylight hours and 12 hours of darkness on both equinoxes. At the other extreme, the sun at the North Pole lies on the horizon of the earth's surface on the March Equinox. The sun rises at noon to the horizon on the March Equinox and the North Pole remains lit until the Autumnal Equinox.

At the exact moment of the equinox, the sun shines directly on the equator before continuing its journey north or south, depending on the time of year. In other words, the equinox is the point in time that the sun crosses the celestial equator. It is an astronomical event that happens simultaneously across the world but is converted into local time. In the Northern Hemisphere, the sun passes over the equator and continues northwards after the Spring Equinox. On the Autumnal Equinox, the sun crosses over the equator and continues its southward declination. In the Southern hemisphere, the path of the sun is reversed. This means that the sun moves south of the equator after the Spring Equinox and will continue its journey north after the Autumnal Equinox.

The Spring Equinox marks the first day of spring in the Northern Hemisphere, the beginning of Aries season, and the celebration of the old pagan holiday, *Ostara*. During the equinox, the sun moves north along the celestial equator. It's a moment in time when we honour the recent journey around the sun. During the celebration, witches will embrace both the solar and lunar energy of the universe by paying tribute to the earth and its beauty. They acknowledge Mother Earth for her bounty of life and food she's given to us all, as well as the balance of all cosmos and celestial energy of the universe. If you want to honour the Equinox, here are some ways to celebrate by zodiac sign according to *TeenVogue* and others:

Aries: Being that the equinox marks the beginning of our solar return (the place the sun was at the exact moment of our birth), it's the perfect time to treat ourselves. Make a flower wreath to embrace abundance and power, using bright seasonal blossoms such as daffodils, camellias, branches, grasses, leaves, and primroses. Gather some flowers from the garden and go wild!

Taurus: Combine two of our favorite things together during the equinox: friends and food. Host a dinner party via Zoom, Teams or FaceTime – just because we can't be physically together right now doesn't mean we can't interact. Light some candles and enjoy fresh vegetables as we usher in the spring together.

Gemini: Our inquisitive mind will want to debunk magical theories, or prove them to be legit. There's nothing to say that we can't mix science and magic. Geminis are flexible, extroverted, and clever, and there's never a boring moment while they're around.

Cancer: The equinox will mark the end of our winter hibernation and kick off days in the sun. Plan an evening out with friends for the future, perhaps a mini bonfire by the beach once we're able to gather again, or a night with a patio fire under the stars to reflect on the past and plan our long-awaited re-entrance on the scene.

Leo: We'll want to run wild during the equinox, which is why it's ideal for us to take a long nature hike alone. Also, our head will clear with the sun's warmth, giving us the motivation and inspiration to manifest our next big creative project.

Virgo: We're known to be a penny pincher, but it's time we spent some of our hard-earned cash on a gift for ourselves. Update our look or the aesthetic of our personal space. Treat ourselves to a fabulous outfit, shoes, makeup, or drapes. After all, we've earned it!

Libra: It's time for us to restore balance in our life. This means finding the right rhythms and routines for our body, mind, and spirit. Take a time out from relationships and situations that don't make us feel we're on level ground and focus our energies around centering ourselves. This will make us feel more at ease.

Scorpio: The equinox is a time of new beginnings. There's no better way to celebrate than to set future intentions with friends and family. Journal some goals for the future, and share them with our friends via text.'

Sagittarius: Become a believer in 'other worlds" by evoking the elementals: Salamanders (fire), gnomes (earth), sylphs (air), and undines (water). Connect to their energy, by meditating near their element, to expand our spiritual power during this energetically potent time of year.

Capricorn: We'll want to stay indoors during *Ostara*, which is why it's a great time for some good old fashioned spring cleaning. Just be sure to donate the items that we don't want (like last season's boots) to a local charity shop.

Aquarius: Our airy spirit will want to get outside on the holiday. Trying our hand at gardening and pot, plant, or trim some blossoms. This activity will allow us to embrace the sun and nature at the same time.

Pisces: Evoke our creative spirit during the equinox by painting or dyeing eggs with spring colours and glitter. *Ostara*, which is considered to be the pagan's Easter, is a time of embracing the life cycle of earth and loving beings (which is represented by the egg). This activity will boost our artistic side, as well as bringing us together with others.

Although it's becoming more popular in the West, the Chinese Spring Festival or New Year date changes each year – always falling between 21st January and 20th February and is determined by the Chinese lunar calendar and the appearance of the New Moon. Marking the end of winter and the beginning of the spring season, observances traditionally take place from New Year's Eve, the evening preceding the first day of the year to the Lantern Festival, held on the 15th day of the year.

Chinese New Year is one of the most important holidays in China, and has strongly influenced Eastern New Year celebrations such as the *Losar* of Tibet, and of China's neighbouring cultures, including Korea and the *Tết* of Vietnam. It is also celebrated worldwide in regions and countries that house significant overseas Chinese populations, Taiwan, Singapore, Indonesia, Malaysia, Myanmar, Thailand, Cambodia, the Philippines, Mauritius, and Canada as well as in North America and Europe.

The Chinese New Year is associated with several myths

and customs. The festival was traditionally a time to honour deities as well as Ancestors. Within China, regional customs and traditions concerning the celebration of the New Year vary widely, and the evening preceding New Year's Day is frequently regarded as an occasion for Chinese families to gather for the annual reunion dinner. It is also traditional for every family to thoroughly clean their house, in order to sweep away any ill-fortune and to make way for incoming good luck.

The Chinese zodiac, or *Sheng Xiao*, is a repeating 12-year cycle of animal signs and their ascribed attributes, based on the lunar calendar. Perhaps the most widespread theory focuses on the legendary Jade Emperor. It's said that he invited all the world's animals to a banquet, but only 12 turned up. As a result, he decided to honour these 12 animals – now popularly known as the 12 Chinese zodiac animals – by dedicating one year on the Chinese calendar to each. Yet another Chinese story claims that the Buddha himself called for 12 sacred animals to protect his palace. He thus organized a race that involved all animals on earth to identify the worthiest. Finally, the top 12 finishers in the race were selected as his guards, who now represent the 12 Chinese zodiac signs. In order, the zodiac animals are: Rat, Ox, Tiger, Rabbit, Dragon, Snake, Horse, Goat, Monkey, Rooster, Dog, Pig.

Animal Personality Traits

Rat: quick-witted, smart, charming, and persuasive
Ox: patient, kind, stubborn, and conservative
Tiger: authoritative, emotional, courageous, and intense
Rabbit: popular, compassionate, and sincere
Dragon: energetic, fearless, warm-hearted, and charismatic
Snake: charming, gregarious, introverted, generous, and smart
Horse: energetic, independent, impatient, and enjoy traveling
Sheep: mild-mannered, shy, kind, and peace-loving

Monkey: fun, energetic, and active

Rooster: independent, practical, hard-working, and observant

Dog: patient, diligent, generous, faithful, and kind

Pig: loving, tolerant, honest, and appreciative of luxury

The Spring Festival, marks the transition from one animal to the next – 2021 was the year of the Ox, which began on 12th February 2021, and ended on 1st February 2022. Chinese New Year 2022 will signal the start of the year of the Tiger and, because the dates of Chinese New Year change every year, individuals born in January or February will need to pay special attention to their birth date in addition to their birth year.

Maybe you think your zodiac year will be lucky. It's *your* year after all. Nevertheless, it's the total opposite because it's seen as a hurdle you have jump over. The way to protect yourself from evil spirits and bad fortune is to wear red underwear every day for the entire year. Even in modern times, it's still treated as a real concern. In some places, married men even have to be accompanied by their wives when they go out at night during their year!

Today is the first day of spring and the Vernal Equinox! An old myth claims we can stand an egg on its end ONLY during the Vernal Equinox, when day and night are equal in length. Supposedly, this is because there is equal gravity between the Earth and the sun on that day. But that's a myth! In reality, we can stand an egg on end any day. Why?

On the bottom of an egg we will find tiny bumps in the shell. Those bumps are simply irregularities in the eggshell that hold the egg up (similar to legs). And, to prove this point, the Children's Museum of Indianapolis demonstrated successfully balancing an egg outside – a full day *before* the Vernal Equinox.

Also, while they were having fun with eggs, they tested out the strength of an egg. Because of the shape of an egg, it can hold up to five pounds of weight on top without breaking! Don't believe it? This is a fun science experiment we can try at home, too in order to amuse our younger guests ...

We will need:

2 caps from 2-liter bottles of fizzy drink
1 egg
hardback books

Process:

Place one bottle cap open-side up on a smooth, level surface.

Put the large end of the egg on the bottle cap.

Put the other cap, open-side down, on the egg.

Gradually add some books or other weighty materials.

More egg trivia

- Spin an egg to see if it's hard-cooked or raw. If it wobbles, it's raw!
- The expression: "It's so hot you could fry an egg on the pavement,' could only be true if the paving reached a temperature of 300°F.
- Eggs have tiny pores just like human skin. Through these pores they can absorb flavors and odors, so it's best to store eggs in a carton in a refrigerator.
- Eggs age more in one day at room temperature than in one week in the refrigerator.
- If you accidentally drop an egg on the floor, sprinkle it with a lot of salt before you clean it up. This makes clean-up easier.

All over the world eggs symbolize the release of earth from winter and the coming of new life in the spring. We hope you enjoy the first day of spring! [The Children's Museum]

The Equinox reminds us that even though we may perceive light and dark as being separate, they only exist because of each other. When we embrace this idea of holistic oneness, we can mindfully check in with ourselves ... body, mind and heart and the constant changing experiences we have during the season, because the end of winter can sometimes feel a little rocky. The energy shifting from an inward-focus to outwardly-focused can make us feel a bit off-kilter.

Implementing changes required in order to grow and flourish, can really disrupt our sense of equilibrium in late winter. But with the Spring Equinox, the Earth returns to a place of perfect balance – day & night are equal, the light and the dark – bringing the return of some much-needed balance into our own lives. And, because this is the season of illumination, spring brings clarity. This is the time to get really clear on what we want to see grow in our life and what we want to reap later in the year. In order to gain that clarity we need to try to find out what's calling us.

Spring and summer bring powerful growth energy. If we're not clear on where to focus that energy, it can feel chaotic and overwhelming. Many of us have learned that our energy gets pulled in many different directions and it can burn us out. In order to gain that clarity, this month try out new ideas and connect with early spring's playful, curious spirit. Look closely at what seeds we wish to plant and decide what we want to achieve in the months ahead. [*Seasonal Soul*]

Prepare a Family Feast

No spring celebration is complete without a family meal filled with seasonal spring foods to go along with it. For the Equinox, celebrate with foods that honour the coming of spring – eggs, early spring greens, shoots, sprouts, seasonal local produce, local bread, wine, etc. Spend some time with our family shopping at our local farmers' market or produce stall to collect local spring foods to prepare for our spring feast! We can finally say goodbye to the long, cold nights of winter and get ready to see the sun again. The Spring Equinox officially marks the start of the spring season, and with it brings a chance to create colourful, veggie-filled meals that will help us shake off those winter blues.

Many on the path of pagan faith, feel that attunement with the seasons is an important component of their beliefs. Is it a tradition of old? Or a rather new invention – this Wheel of the Year, this celebration of the stations of the Sun? Being one with the turn of the seasons has definitely been an essential feature since the Neolithic era, when nomadic hunter-gatherers turned into farmers. Maybe the seasons weren't actually celebrated back then because they were such an integral part of life anyway.

To be honest, at least in the European culture in which I grew up, *everything* was about food. Even when sitting at the table enjoying the food in front of us, we'd talk about it ... but not only that. Food played a big role in our Ancestor's lives, too. There were laws about who was to sit where at the table, who got their food on what kind of dishes, and who got which cut of the meat. Food found its way not only into law, but also into literature. In the stories of the Welsh *Mabinogi*, thirteen banquets are mentioned, some described in much detail, and we encounter phrases similar to 'going to feast' over sixty times in the text! And, I'm still very much a 'foodie' to this present day.

For our Vernal Equinox celebration, we should prepare a meal of traditional, seasonal dishes. Even TV-Chef Jamie Oliver has included wild garlic soup on his blog page by Ren Behan, a well-known food writer and mum-of-two based in Hertfordshire. She also grew up in a food-loving Polish household and now writes a popular family-friendly and seasonally-inspired blog.

Wild garlic might sound like a rare ingredient only used in posh restaurants, but it's actually one of the most commonly foraged edible leaves and it can be found growing in abundance, in the woodlands, at this time of year. Wild garlic can also be known as ramsons, bear's garlic or wood garlic. It grows from late winter until around the end of May. Towards the end of its season, it produces pretty, small white flowers. The flowers are edible, too.

Wild garlic is related to chives and can be used in the same way as you would use baby spinach or a delicate herb, such as basil. If you rub the leaves between your fingers, you should get a strong smell of garlic. The leaves are very delicate and only taste mildly garlicky. You can eat them raw, and are great when added to a big salad served with a plate of pasta or a lasagne. If you are making a stir-fry for supper, quickly chop your wild garlic and add it towards the end of cooking. You could also shred the leaves and add them to a soup as a garnish, or to an omelette with herbs or even a quiche or savoury tart.

At this time of year, as spring veggies also come into season, I like to make a big pan of vegetable risotto, simply stirring some wild garlic leaves through at the end. Or, you could whizz the leaves up with pine nuts, parmesan and olive oil to make a quick wild garlic pesto to stir through your risotto or pasta dish. You could also try adding some finely shredded leaves to some softened, fresh butter to make garlic butter, and use it spread over a pizza base or ciabatta for a milder-tasting garlic bread that the kids will really love.

Wild Garlic Soup

Ingredients:

4 Cups Beef broth
2 Hands full wild garlic leaves (or 2 stalks of leek)
2 Tbsp butter
1 Tbsp flour
1 small onion, finely chopped
Salt
White pepper
½ to 1 Cup heavy cream

Process:

Blanch the wild garlic leaves and set aside. Melt the butter in the soup pot; add the finely chopped onion and sauté over medium heat until glassy. Add the flour and stir continuously to avoid clumps. Keep sautéing until the flour turns ever so slightly yellow. Pour in the liquid while still stirring. Let simmer for 10 minutes. Now add the blanched wild garlic leaves – except for two or three – to the soup, then the heavy cream. When the soup is done, purée it with a blender (immersion if available). Cut the remaining whole wild garlic leaves in fine stripes and use them as garnish when serving.

Lamb is the meat of the season because it is plentiful but I always prefer my lamb to be a year old and have had the sun on its back ... Welsh lamb is meat from sheep breeds that are born and reared in Wales and is firm and white with good colour and has a sweet, succulent flavour. It is sold as fresh meat, either as whole body or leg, shoulder, loin, saddle or cutlets.

Cig Oen A Mel – Honeyed Lamb

Ingredients:

3-4 lb shoulder of spring lamb
2 level tablespoons rosemary
Salt and freshly ground black pepper
1 teaspoon ginger
8 oz (1 cup generous) thick honey
½ pint (1 cup) cider approx

Process:

First line the baking tine with foil, as the honey can make it very sticky. Rub the shoulder all over with salt, pepper and the ginger, then put into the baking tin and sprinkle half the finely chopped rosemary over the top. Coat the top skin with honey and pour the cider around. Bake in a hot oven (400°F) for ½ hour then lower the heat to 323°F and cook for a further 1¼ hours. Fifteen minutes before it is ready baste carefully and sprinkle over the remaining rosemary. Add a little more cider if it appears to be drying up. Pour off any excess fat from the gravy and reduce slightly on top of the stove, adding more cider if it has evaporated. Serve the sauce separately in a warmed gravy boat. [*A Taste of Wales*]

Rhubarb Fool Dessert

This is a classic British dessert that's an easy delight you need to try. Light, creamy, tart and full of flavour, it shows rhubarb off at its finest, while bringing back memories of childhood in the most delicious way. Rhubarb fool is a classic British dessert made with stewed rhubarb and whipped cream. Some versions use just cream, while others use some yogurt mixed in. Another take is a custard fool using *creme Anglaise* ('real' custard), though that's arguably a different dessert to some. It's incredibly simple, and such a delicious treat as the soft, slightly tart fruit and smooth cream mingle together. Gently cook the fruit first to bring out their flavors and, for tarter fruits, lightly sweeten them. Don't add much liquid as it will create its own and the fruit should stay relatively intact.

The contrast in rich cream and sweet-tart fruit is what makes this dish. The trick in blending this together is not completely combining the fruit and cream, but more 'folding' them together. This way you can still get the flavor and texture of both coming through. One of the other great things about this dessert, as well as being so easy, is that it can be made part or fully ahead of time. You can cook the fruit a few days ahead and then simply refrigerate in a container until needed. Although it's best not to make it too far ahead as the air will start to come out of the cream and so it loses its lightness. Plus, the acidity of the fruit can seep into the cream making it a bit liquid. However, it can certainly be made it a few hours ahead and just cover and refrigerate. It makes a great dessert for entertaining guests after a substantial meal.

In rural Britain, it was traditional to drink dandelion and burdock cordials at the Vernal Equinox because these herbs were believed to help to cleanse the blood and are a good tonic for the body after its winter hardships. Dandelion is purported to boot immunity and reduce inflammation; burdock root is known as an antioxidant that clears toxins from the blood – but there have been countless other slightly more dubious uses noted through the centuries, from curing baldness to reducing fever with a poultice on the feet. [Blackthorn & Stone Blog]

There are eight annual sacred days in Celtic mythology: *Imbolc, Beltane, Lughnasadh, Samhain,* two equinoxes, and two solstices. Many ancient Irish mythological traditions surrounding these sacred days disappeared during the 20th century, but neo-pagans and historians have used ancient records and documented observations to piece together the traditions and revive the ceremonies. Like *Imbolc,* the Spring Equinox was adopted by the church and associated with St. Patrick, Ireland's first patron saint, which is celebrated annually on 17th March. Ancient Celts saw this balance in nature as an indication of the presence of magic and, in the case of the Spring Equinox, a time to sow seeds.

Needless to say, a bonfire is a great way to celebrate the Vernal Equinox since this is one of the sacred fire festivals and our Ancestors believed that the successful progression of the year relied heavily on sacred rituals observed on both solstices and equinoxes, accompanied by telling stories, dancing, singing, beating drums, playing music, and celebrating the spring. With patches of snow still covering the ground in parts of Britain, it may not seem like the first day of spring but, as of today, winter is officially over for another year.

At night (dusk), bonfires are lit and entertaining games bring comfort to everyone by helping to brighten the space between the earth and the spiritual world. A time full of magic and divination, spells of protection, love, prosperity, and cleansing are performed hand in hand with more formal rituals. Celebrating the fire festivals can vary from one witch to another. Sprinkling a touch of our own personality would be ideal as this celebration embraces diversity and gives room for personal growth and elevation as we welcome in the spring by the blaze from our own fire-pit.

- Also take a private moment to celebrate the new life beginning that surrounds us in nature by watching the sunrise and/or sunset on this special day.
- And since there is nothing like the fresh smell and beauty of spring in the house, pick or purchase several bouquets of seasonal flowers to decorate your home.

Chapter Three

Ostara

The word Oestra originates from the name of the goddess Eostre. In the past, pagans held a huge festival to honor Eostre on *the same day* that Easter falls today – on the first Sunday *after* the first full moon that falls *after* the Spring Equinox. I know it's a mouthful, but it is still the date chosen to be 'Easter' to this very day!

Easter gets its name from the Teutonic goddess of spring and the dawn, whose name is spelled *Oestre* or *Eastre*. Modern pagans have generally accepted the spelling *Ostara* (Oh-star-ah), which honors this goddess as the focus for the Vernal Equinox – but the evidence for Ostara as an *actual* goddess people worshipped is sketchy. We can pin her down in the writings of an 8th century monk, the Venerable Bede, who reported that pagan Anglo-Saxons in medieval Northumbria held festivals in Ostara's honour during the month of *Eostremonath* (April). However, some have speculated that he was making this up (or at least embellishing the truth) as he went along!

As a holiday, Easter predates Christianity and was originally the name for the Spring Equinox – but as Christianity spread through Northern Europe and people maintained their older traditions, the church started to encompass these pagan customs and festivals within the Christian calendar. It is said that St Patrick (whose feast day is also celebrated around the Spring Equinox) very deliberately incorporated Irish folk traditions and beliefs into Christian practice as he actively converted the population of Ireland. For example, the Celtic cross features a circle at the centre – as the sun was venerated within the Irish pagan tradition, St Patrick thought that this would help his converts associate the cross with divinity. Considering how popular the Celtic cross is today, it seems this campaign was a success.

Fixing the date on which the Resurrection of Jesus was to be observed and celebrated triggered a major controversy in early Christianity in which both an Eastern and a Western position can be distinguished. The dispute, known as the 'Paschal controversies', was not definitively resolved until the 8th century. In 325CE, the Council of Nicaea decreed that Easter should be observed on the first Sunday following the first full moon after the spring equinox (21st March), which means that Easter can fall on any Sunday between 22nd March and 25th April ... Eastern Orthodox churches use a slightly different calculation based on the old Julian rather than the Gregorian calendar (which is now thirteen days ahead of the former), with the result that the Orthodox Easter celebration usually occurs later than that celebrated by Protestants and Roman Catholics.

In the 20th century several attempts were made to arrive at a fixed date for Easter, with the Sunday following the second Saturday in April specifically proposed. While this proposal and others had many supporters, none came to fruition. Renewed interest in a fixed date arose in the early 21st century, resulting from discussions involving the leaders of Eastern Orthodox, Syriac Orthodox, Coptic, Anglican, and Roman Catholic churches, but formal agreement on such a date remained elusive!

Easter, like Christmas, has accumulated a great many traditions, some of which have little to do with the actual Christian celebration of the Resurrection but derive from assorted folk customs. The custom of the Easter lamb appropriates both the appellation used for Jesus in Scripture and the lamb's role as a sacrificial animal in ancient Israel. In antiquity Christians placed lamb meat under the altar, had it blessed, and then ate it on Easter. Since the 12th century the Lenten fast has ended on Easter with meals including eggs, ham, cheeses, bread, and sweets that have been blessed for the occasion. [Britannica]

The custom of associating a rabbit or 'bunny' with Easter arose in Protestant areas in Europe in the 17th century but did not become common until the 19th century. The Easter rabbit is said to lay the eggs as well as decorate and hide them. In the United States the Easter rabbit also leaves children baskets with toys and candies on Easter morning. In a way, this was a manifestation of the Protestant rejection of Catholic Easter customs. In some European countries, however, other animals – in Switzerland the cuckoo, in Westphalia the fox – brought the Easter eggs.

Which takes care of the Christian concept of Easter and allows those of pagan persuasion to re-appropriate the festival as yet another of our own that had been expropriated by the church for their convenience.

The Spring Equinox for pagans, is a time for rituals and celebrations surrounding the themes of fertility, new beginnings, and rebirth. Eggs and bunnies represent fertility, while eggs and seedlings are considered symbols of rebirth and renewal. In ancient times, baskets filled with eggs were offered to Eostre as a symbol of fertility and new beginnings.

Since Easter is celebrated on the same day that the pre-Christians celebrated Eostre, many of the traditions associated with Eostre and the Spring Equinox have been reinvented and included in contemporary traditions. It is, therefore, no coincidence that the word Easter is very similar to the word Eostre. Easter baskets, coloured or dyed eggs, and even the Easter 'bunny' became a way to continue to honour the rituals and traditions that the masses found most meaningful. This is why many of the rituals and customs that were once associated with the Spring Equinox have become an integral part of the generic Easter traditions today.

More importantly, for most of us, it's probably safe to say we're all aware that an Easter holiday is a timely idea but just what *are* the actual benefits? Let us have a look at some research findings and scientific facts which establish exactly why we should prioritise a family holiday, from strengthening relationships to improving our health. Just in case we needed any other excuses to getaway and the Easter holidays became an acceptable part of family life for those of the 'baby boomer' generation. We hadn't got around to the cut price package trips but a long-weekend under canvass wasn't a bad alternative. The Easter scout-camp at the Quarries, surrounded by hawthorn trees in blossom, is still one of my sharpest childhood memories.

If nothing else, it established the idea that a family holiday should be all about treating ourselves to a refreshing break from the normal habits and day-to-day life. According to an article published in *TES* by Elizabeth Buie, a staggering two thirds of conversations between parents and children revolve around their daily routine. A holiday away provides the perfect opportunity to break this conversation cycle and provide more engaging exchanges between parents and children – plus it gives us more time to get to know their individual personalities and notice how they're growing, changing and developing as *people* at all ages.

Taking a step away from the established family routine whilst on holiday may help us to spot what is (or indeed isn't) working in our regular patterns at home; providing us with the foresight to see how changes might be implemented upon our return. This kind of thinking can have a really positive impact on how the family interacts and communicates while on holiday, and of course, once we're back at home.

Time away from the stresses, work commitments and time constraints of day-to-day home life allows us much more free time on holiday to reconnect and enjoy hanging out as a family. In light of a sobering statistic in a *Daily Telegraph* article which cites that 65% of parents say they only play with their children occasionally, we should definitely grab the opportunity on holiday to play lots more! Play should be a crucial part of childhood as it helps kids learn patience, improves their problem-solving skills and encourages creativity. Spending time playing with children also reinforces the idea that they are loved and appreciated.

Playing is important for adults too! Since a third of fathers apparently say they don't have time to play with their children and one in six fathers say they don't know *how* to play with their child, according to a Playmobil UK survey. It's also worth remembering that playing has the same benefits for grown-ups. It'll work the same cognitive skills as children, such as problem solving and creativity, whilst also acting as a massive stress reliever and help us feel more connected with our kids. Research from the Family Holiday Association has shown that 49% of Brits have created their happiest memories whilst being on holiday with their family.

Family holidays takes us out of our usual routine and this tends to mean our surroundings and experiences make a deeper impact on our consciousness. Fun family times together creates good memories and, according to research featured on the BBC, positive memories are scientifically proven to stick around for longer than bad ones. Furthermore, nearly a quarter (24%) of people surveyed said that they call on these happy memories when times get tough. I still have stronger memories of family holidays than of those taken in later years. Time to start having lots more fun it seems!

Family holidays are healthy! Focusing on our physical health is becoming ever more front-of-mind for most of us, but research (Holt-Lunsted, 2015) highlighted that our 'relationship health' also has a massive impact on our physical health. Family holidays can improve relationships between family members with improved communication, relaxed time together and the joy of shared experiences. In addition, family holidays naturally tend to involve 'green exercise' i.e. being active outdoors – which has been proven to give mental and physical wellbeing a real boost. Connecting with nature, by all accounts, has a whole heap of benefits – from improving our mood and giving us a confidence boost, right through to helping our body produce more virus and tumour fighting white blood cells.

Family holidays also provide the perfect opportunity to strengthen (or indeed rebuild) relationships between loved ones. Research shows only one in four children talk to their parents about 'something that matters' more than once a week. A family holiday gives us the time and relaxed setting to chat about things other than day-to-day chores, homework or what's for dinner. Although technology means we're more 'in touch' than ever before, nothing beats physical time together. Spending close time with family members gives us the chance to develop a much closer understanding of each other through body language, subtle nuances, gestures and facial expressions that just aren't possible via text or WhatsApp! [Neilson]

All in all, spending time together as a family on holiday simply provides us all with the opportunity to enjoy each other's company, giving each other the reassurance we are loved and creating fabulous memories for us all. After all, the years go by quickly enough and all too often the scrimmage of life gets in the way of those shared moments.

The Easter Egg Hunt

In many different cultures, eggs held associations with spring and new life. Early Christians adapted these beliefs, making the egg a symbol of the resurrection and the empty shell a metaphor for Jesus' tomb.

In the medieval period eating eggs was forbidden during Lent, the forty day period before Easter. On Easter Sunday the fast ended with feasting and merriment, and eggs were considered an important part of these celebrations. This was especially true for poorer people who couldn't afford meat. Eggs were also given to the church as Good Friday offerings, and villagers often gave eggs as gifts to the lord of the manor at Easter. Royals got involved with this tradition too – in 1290 Edward I purchased 450 eggs to be decorated with colours or gold leaf and then distributed to his household.

The custom of the Easter egg hunt, however, comes from Germany. Some suggest that its origins date back to the late 16th century, when the Protestant reformer Martin Luther organised egg hunts for his congregation. The men would hide the eggs for the women and children to find. In the German Lutheran tradition the Easter egg hunt was linked to the Easter Bunny – or the Easter Hare as he was originally known. The first written reference to the Easter Hare was in 1682 in Georg Franck von Franckenau's essay, *De ovis paschalibus* ('About Easter Eggs'). Links between Easter hares and rabbits, however, go back earlier in central Europe. Custom had it that the hare would bring a basket of brightly painted eggs for all the children who had been good, and these would be hidden around the house and garden for the children to find.

As a child, the future Queen Victoria enjoyed egg hunts at Kensington Palace. These were arranged by her mother, the German-born Duchess of Kent. On Sunday, 7th April 1833, the 14-year-old Princess Victoria wrote in her diary: 'Mama did some pretty painted & ornamented eggs, & we looked for them'. Victoria and Albert continued this German tradition of hiding eggs for their own children to find on Maundy Thursday. Albert was responsible for hiding the eggs, concealing them in 'little moss baskets' and hiding them around the palace. Victoria made numerous references to these egg hunts in her journals, including in 1869 when she wrote: 'After breakfast, the children, as usual on this day looked for Easter eggs.'

The eggs were probably hard-boiled and decorated, as was the custom at the time. The simplest way to colour eggs was to boil them with onion skins, which gave the shells a rich golden hue.

Another technique was to wrap the egg in gorse flowers before boiling. This produced a delicate yellow and brown pattern.

Though the egg hunt had its origins in central Europe, Britain had its own egg-related Easter traditions. In the north of England and in Scotland the custom of decorating eggs, and giving them as presents, or using them to decorate the home goes back many centuries. Known as 'pace-egging' from the Latin for Easter, *pascha*, it is first recorded in early 18th century Lancashire, and by the early 19th century was popular across large parts of the country.

Egg rolling was also an Easter tradition in the north of Britain, particularly in Cumbria, where children came together from the 1790s to roll decorated eggs down grassy hills. In the Edwardian period large crowds gathered each year at traditional egg rolling sites like the castle moat at Penrith, Avenham Park in Preston, and Arthur's Seat in Edinburgh.

Easter eggs and the egg hunt became more popular in mainstream England in the late 19th and early 20th centuries as society began to change. Family life became more of a priority for the expanding Victorian middle classes, and they had more disposable income. The Victorians were also fascinated by old traditions. As a result, Easter moved away from being a primarily religious and communal celebration and became more centred on family, home and the pleasures of children. Nevertheless, at the turn of the century egg hunts remained something of a novelty – so much so that in 1892 the poet A.E. Housman thought it was worth noting that 'In Germany at Easter time they hide coloured eggs about the house and garden that the children may amuse themselves in discovering them.' But since the mid-20th century, confectionery companies such as Fry's, Cadbury's and Rowntree have used the popularity of Easter egg hunts to promote their products. [English Heritage]

A Family That Eats Together, Stays Together

Dinner time is family time. Suppers eaten with mum and dad, or other significant adults in a child's life, have been shown to have much more than just nutritional value. So, next time you're grabbing a take-out to eat in the back of the car on the way to hockey practice, keep these things in mind – and make Easter Sunday a very special lunch.

Ostara is our pagan celebration of Spring: it's the time of year when new life is beginning to form, and fresh little green things are starting to poke their way out of the chilly earth. If were really lucky, we may be able to find some spring greens to nibble on! Looking for recipes to brighten up our Ostara celebration? Check out where to find information on seasonal treats such as eggs, breads, salads, and desserts for the occasion. For example – during the pre-Easter season of Lent, many of our Christian friends and family members are busily enjoying traditional hot cross buns.

This is a spicy pastry that's been around for a long time, and the decorative cross on the top represents one of the most obvious symbols of Christianity. There are, however, a number of English traditions revolving around them. One custom says that sailors should take a hot cross bun on their travels to prevent shipwreck. The cross on the bun comes from a superstition that marking the bun so would prevent the Devil from getting into the baked goods. Interestingly, it's possible that breads with crosses on top were baked by the ancient Greeks, which makes the whole idea pre-Christian anyway.

So, how can we incorporate a hot cross bun into our pagan belief system? Well, what sort of things appear in fours in your tradition? Here are some things that the four quarters of the cross could represent, depending on what matters most to each of us. [Learn Religions]

- The four elements: Choose a quarter to represent each of the four elements of earth, air, fire and water.
- The four directions: Many Pagan traditions place an emphasis on the directions of north, east, south and west.
- The four phases of the moon: Select each quarter to symbolize the dark moon, the waxing moon, the full moon and the waning phase.
- The four seasons: Each quadrant could be representative of spring, summer, fall, and winter.
- The fire feasts or quarter festivals: The Fire Festivals, or cross quarter days, include *Imbolc, Beltane, Lammas/ Lughnasadh*, and *Samhain*. The Quarter festivals, or lesser sabbats, include the solstices and equinoxes.
- The four suits of the Tarot: Each section can symbolize Wands, Cups, Coins or Swords.

And nothing need go to waste because stale hot cross buns are just as enjoyable toasted. In fact, keep some in the freezer to be used for afternoon tea on a damp, chilly day – served with real butter and jam.

Easter Sunday Lunch

Devilled Eggs

Did you know that the phrase 'deviled', when used to refer to food, has nothing to do with devils at all? It was apparently coined during the late 18th century, when it was applied to any food item that was hot or spicy. Deviled eggs are supremely easy to make, and you can make them sweet or spicy. This recipe is for a tangy, spicy version of the classic spring dish. Make this delicious egg starter for your Ostara get-togethers and celebrations.

Ingredients:

1 dozen eggs
1 tbsp. Dijon mustard
1/4 cup mayonnaise
1 tsp. curry powder
1/2 tsp. white vinegar
Salt and pepper to taste
Paprika
Parsley, for garnish

Preparation:

Hard-boil the eggs and allow them to cool before peeling. Peel the eggs and slice each one in half lengthwise. Remove the yolks and place them in a bowl. Mash the yolks up with a fork, and add the Dijon mustard, mayonnaise, curry powder, vinegar and salt and pepper. Blend it all together. Gently spoon the yolk mixture into the white halves, and sprinkle with paprika. Garnish with parsley sprigs for serving.

For our ancestors, lamb was the first real meat they got each year, after the cold winter months. Ostara is the time of the spring lambs, and if you're a meat eater, a marinated and roasted leg of lamb is the perfect dish for your Spring Equinox celebrations. Or preparing a succulent roast chicken for the Easter Sunday lunch, because a roasted chicken is the perfect meal for a crowd since it is affordable, tasty, and easy to make. Fill the house with the smell of a home-cooked meal this Easter Sunday. This recipe pairs well with many white wines, especially a rich and buttery Chardonnay. Serve with side dishes such as steamed green beans, mashed potatoes, and fresh baked rolls. Here's a recipe for a delicious citrus and herb roasted chicken – the perfect dish for your holiday celebration [Punchbowl]

Citrus & Herb Roasted Chicken

Ingredients:

1 whole roasting chicken (5 to 6 lbs.),
neck and giblets discarded
1 orange, quartered
1 lemon, quartered
1 head garlic (halved) plus 3 garlic cloves (chopped)
2 (14 oz.) cans reduced-sodium chicken broth
¼ cup frozen orange juice concentrate, thawed
¼ cup fresh lemon juice
2 tbsp. olive oil
Salt and freshly ground black pepper
1 tbsp. chopped fresh oregano leaves
Kitchen string (or butcher twine)

Process:

Preheat oven to 400º F and make sure rack is in the center of the oven. Pat the chicken dry and sprinkle with salt and pepper. Stuff the chicken with the orange, lemon, and garlic halves. Tie the chicken legs together with kitchen string to help hold its shape. Sprinkle with more salt and pepper. Place a rack in a large roasting pan. Place the chicken, breast side up, on the rack in the pan. Roast the chicken for 1 hour. Baste occasionally and add some chicken broth to the pan, if necessary. This is to prevent the pan drippings from burning. Whisk the orange juice, lemon juice, oil, oregano, and chopped garlic in a medium bowl until blended. Brush some of the juice mixture over the chicken, after it has baked 1 hour. Continue to roast the chicken until a meat thermometer inserted into the innermost part of the thigh reads 170º F. Baste occasionally with the juice mixture and add broth to the pan, about 45 minutes longer. Once cooked through, transfer the chicken to a platter.

This dessert recipe could not be any more Easter if it tried! What a way to use up hot cross buns from BBC Food Half a broken-up chocolate eggs can be sprinkled over the buns before placing in the oven if desired.

Ingredients:

6 hot cross buns, halved
butter, for spreading
600ml/20fl oz milk
400ml/14fl oz double cream
1 cinnamon stick
4 free-range eggs
1 tsp vanilla extract
150g/5½oz caster sugar
vanilla ice cream or custard to serve

Method:

Preheat the oven to 180C/160C Fan/Gas 4. Spread butter on each half of hot cross bun and arrange the buns in a large ovenproof dish. Gently heat the milk and cream together in a saucepan with the cinnamon stick. Remove from the heat to cool slightly. Whisk the eggs together with the vanilla and sugar until pale, then gradually pour in the milk and cream mixture, whisking constantly. Remove the cinnamon stick, then pour the mixture over the hot cross buns and allow to soak in for 15 minutes. Place the ovenproof dish in a large baking tray filled halfway up with water. Sprinkle the chocolate pieces over the top and bake for 45 minutes. Serve hot with vanilla ice cream or custard on the side.

Give the house a festive feel throughout with numerous bowls of daffodils and sweet-smelling hyacinths but don't gamble on the weather being warm enough to sit outside, especially if we're catering for elderly parents/grandparents. As usual, many of us will be looking forward to celebrating Easter in the garden with our nearest and dearest – probably despite the uncertain weather forecast. Food editor Alison Oakervee shares her tips for an outside Easter celebration to remember, come rain or shine (or even snow). All you need is warming food, loved ones and a dash of good old British spirit

> In this country, good weather is never guaranteed – I've definitely had my fair share of soggy barbecues and drizzly picnics. When the forecast is chilly, I provide each guest with their own blanket and hot water bottle – they make such a difference, and give a cosy 'ski chalet' vibe. Fire pits are great to provide warmth and ambience – if you don't have one, just carefully burn logs in your barbecue.
>
> I always cook a roast at Easter – but if you're entertaining outside, how about a pot roast? Everything's cooked together so there are no fiddly side dishes, and it will stay warmer in the pot, too. The recipes generally contain all the veg you need – just serve with some crusty bread to dip into the delicious juices. For vegetarian guests try a whole pot roasted cauliflower with a tasty tomato sauce? [Waitrose]

Easter is not exactly a sports holiday, which is to say that Easter is in absolutely no way a sports holiday these days, unless you consider hunting (for plastic eggs) a sport. The problem with Easter not being a sports holiday is that, well, the holiday falls on a Sunday where there are *always* sporting events to watch – in reality or on television. Nevertheless, perhaps it's time for those sports enthusiasts to give it a miss for one weekend and concentrate on putting their efforts into making it a great family weekend.

Stoolball

Nevertheless in *Seasonal Feasts & Festivals*, Professor James reveals that around the Easter Festival a number of less strenuous and destructive ball games were enjoyed, such as stoolball played especially by girls and women. Stoolball is attested by name as early as 1450. Nearly all medieval references describe it as a game played during Easter celebrations, typically as a courtship pastime rather than a competitive game. Written by William Shakespeare and the Sussex-born playwright John Fletcher, the comedy, *The Two Noble Kinsmen* used the phrase 'playing stool ball' as a euphemism for sexual behaviour.

> According to the *Oxford English Dictionary*: *Stool-ball, n.* *'An old country game somewhat resembling cricket, played chiefly by young women or, as an Easter game, between young men and women for a 'tansy' [a festive cake or pudding flavoured with tansy flowers] as the stake.'*

Room (and weather) permitting, if there's a large family to be kept amused, why not arrange a team-game so that guests of all ages can participate:

- Stoolball is a traditional team sport, similar to cricket. Two teams compete to score the most runs. There are two square wickets standing at shoulder height, about 14 metres apart. The bats are willow, with a round face and a long, sprung handle. The ball, small and hard, is bowled underarm towards one wicket.
- Just like cricket, batsmen score by hitting the ball into the field and running between the two wickets. They can also hit the ball beyond a boundary line to score 4 or 6. Batsmen can be bowled, caught or run-out, or even body-before-wicket.
- You don't have to be really fit to play, and children start

playing at around 8 or 9, and some people play league stoolball right into their 70s. There are lots of ladies-only teams, as well as mixed teams with six men and five women. In the mixed game there are rules to ensure everyone gets a fair chance: half the overs must be bowled by women and half by men, and usually there's a man and a woman batting together.

- Any large grassy area will do in fine weather because Stoolball doesn't need a perfect pitch and it's quick to set up.
- Stoolball is an ancient English game which has been played for over 500 years and is probably the origin of baseball and cricket too. Once popular right across England, it has been played at Lord's cricket ground and in the gardens of Buckingham Palace, and overseas including Sri Lanka, India and Australia – even on ocean liners!

Why not start a collection of ceramic 'Easter bunnies' to be brought out each year like we do with the Christmas tree decorations and which are greeted like old friends – even by the adults!

Chapter Four

Beltaine

From time immemorial the seasonal sequence has arrested the attention of mankind and aroused an intense emotional reaction in all states and stages of culture and types of society extending from the Upper Paleolithic in prehistoric times to the highest civilizations of the ancient Near East and the Graeco-Roman world, with repercussions on the subsequent development of custom. Belief and behavior in the intervening ages, not least in the folk-cultures in Europe. The reason is not far to seek. Everywhere and at all times the means of subsistence have been the primary concern and from this fundamental requirement recurrent seasonal periodic festivals have sprung, and by constant repetition they have assumed a variety of forms and acquired diverse meanings and interpretations. But since food has always been an essential need it is in this context that the observances have exercised their primary functions. [*Seasonal Feasts & Festivals*]

In Scotland and Ireland, the ancient Celtic practice of lighting bonfires at the beginning of May as part of a sacrificial rite lingered on until the 18th-century in the observance known as *Beltaine*. The name derived from the Gaelic *tein-eigin* – 'need-fire' and the practice of lighting sacred fires, often on hill-tops, at the beginning of the second division of the Celtic year was for the purpose of stimulating the sun as the life-giving agent at the commencement of summer. Thus on the Eve of May Day, branches of rowan of buckthorn were fastened to the houses and cattle-stalls to keep away malevolent spirits, and the gorse was set on fire at the break of day to burn them out. 'Home fires were extinguished and rekindled with appropriate ceremonies –

the antiquity of which custom is indicated by the use of earlier methods of fire-making by friction, tinder and flint and steel being employed for the purpose, according to Professor E O James.

When the *Beltaine* bonfires had been lighted from the need-fire, branches were lit and carried into the houses to ignite the new fires in the grates. In the Highlands of Scotland this was the only occasion when the peat-fires were put out and relighted (by the friction method) like the annual renewal of the sacred fire in the temple of Vesta on 1st March by the Vestal Virgins. That the *Beltaine* fires were regarded as cathartic and regenerative is suggested by the custom of driving cattle through them to protect them from disease.

April's showers will hopefully have given way to rich and fertile earth, and as the land becomes greener, there are few celebrations as representative of fertility and/or regeneration as *Beltaine*. Festivities typically begin the evening before, on the last night of April. It's a time to welcome the abundance of the fertile earth, and a day that has a long (and sometimes colourful) history. This spring celebration is all about new life, fire, passion and rebirth, so there are all kinds of creative ways we can set up for welcoming the season.

There *are* many different ways we can celebrate *Beltaine*, but the focus is nearly always on the fact that it is a major Fire Festival and we need to find ways of incorporating this into our celebrations. A fire pit is primarily ambient/atmospheric, although it can have some warming properties, depending on how powerful it is and how large. It's one of those lovely features for people to gather around in the evening, since it's pleasant in cool, balmy, or even slightly warm weather. Only in downright hot temperatures does the mere look of fire cause discomfort. However, since fire pits are mainly ornamental, if weather is truly frigid or there's a lot of precipitation, a fire pit doesn't really do much to combat the weather and may actually get damaged.

Having a fire pit in our garden will ensure we can enjoy

the outdoors for longer when the sun goes in and, really, who doesn't enjoy sitting and looking at an open fire? Covid restrictions have hopefully been amended, so now we can begin to think of having the family over for a big celebratory 'Beltaine Bash'. If we haven't already invested, a fire pit is a great item to have in our garden for those Fire Festivals, so we can continue with a much-needed me-time behind the garden-gate once the sun's gone in. But what to choose? There are lots of designs but before using your garden fire pit, ensure it's in a safe location and away from any combustible surfaces.

- Make sure that the location is safe and there's nothing hanging nearby that could catch fire.
- Position your outdoor fire pit in the middle of your patio, so you have plenty of room to move around it safely and it's not too close to combustible surfaces, grass, trees, plants or shrubs.
- Make sure that it isn't too close to your property or sheds/summer houses.
- Don't light the fire pit under a gazebo or other covered area.
- Check the wind direction before lighting.
- Take fire safety precautions. For example, have a fire extinguisher, fire blanket or at least a bucket of water/sand nearby.
- Keep children and animals away if they are unsupervised.
- When you have finished with the fire pit, ensure that the fire is completely extinguished. Cover the fire pit with a suitable lid to contain any hot embers and prevent ash from blowing around.
- If you have chosen a fire pit that doesn't have legs or which gets very hot, you may need to protect the surface underneath.

On the evening of 13th May, those of traditional British Old Craft observe the *Beltaine* ritual in compliance with the old Julian calendar, or we may choose a weekend nearest to the 31st April in harmony with the general pagan community. The rite can be as simple or complicated as we like to make it but the basic component is fire, which can be a roaring summer bonfire, a smouldering fire-pit or an open patio fire-basket. We've even taken part in a rite where the fire was contained within a metal bucket with holes knocked in it!

Whether as part of a group, or a solitary working, fire should be an integral part of any *Beltaine* ceremony. Again, the purists would say that the fire should be lit as part of the ritual but there's nothing more embarrassing that being stared at by a group of people eagerly awaiting a cheery blaze while the fire-maker fumbles about with damp matches and even damper kindling that refuses to ignite. *Beltaine* should be a joyous occasion but this kind of enforced gaiety is on a par with those who insist on still holding a family barbeque in the garden when it's pouring with rain because it's been planned for that day!

In modern parlance, in our rites we are basically asking for health, wealth and happiness in the coming days of plenty, i.e. a summer – with plenty of food = health and wealth plus 'mirth and song'. The holiday celebrates spring at its peak, and the coming of summer. This holiday is associated very strongly with fertility/regeneration, but for pagans how does this translate into a generic meaning that all our guests can relate to?

To put the matter in a nut-shell – regeneration is an ambiguous term with diverse meanings. According to the *Oxford English Dictionary*, to be regenerated is to be 're-born; brought again into existence; formed anew', no doubt an accurate usage but one that is arguably too narrow. More appropriate is another meaning the OED suggests: 'restored to a better state' – spiritual renewal or revival. Most definitions of regeneration, however, have been driven, over many times and places, by concern about ageing and the desire, at best, to reverse or, at least, to modify its perceived ill-effects. And as Robert Cochrane once observed, there had been no cause for a fertility religion in Europe since the advent of the coultershare plough in the 13th century!

The May Pole dances are survivals of ancient rituals around a living tree as part of the spring rites to ensure fertility. Over time it usually became a tree trunk of the correct height, age, and type (usually pine or birch). Some writers claim that the tree represented masculine energy, and the ribbons and floral garlands that adorned it represented feminine energy. While those ribbon-weaving dancers are either pairs of boys and girls (with girls taking one colour of ribbons and boys the other), *or* a group of multiple ages where younger dancers take the inside of the circle and older dancers the outside; either way, the maypole itself is a splendid reminder that spring has sprung and regeneration has begun.

Given that May Day celebrations are all about expressive dancing and celebrating, the Puritans in 16th and 17th century New England labeled the rituals 'bacchanalian', which naturally led to the banning of the celebrations during that time. Luckily May Day festivities made their way back into the modern era and remain a symbol of the wondrous shift from the dreary cold season to the lively warmer one. We can find today's most dedicated revelers in Scotland and Ireland, where they recognize *Beltaine* or Gaelic May Day, or in the United Kingdom and Bavaria – where the maypole is painted in their region's white and blue and adorned with representations of the local craftspeople and trades.

The tradition of the Maypole Dance has been around for a long time – it's a celebration of the fertility of the season. Because *Beltaine* festivities usually kicked off the night before with a big bonfire, the Maypole celebration usually took place shortly after sunrise the next morning. Young people came and danced around the pole, each holding the end of a ribbon. As they wove in and out, men going one way and women the other, it created a sleeve of sorts – the enveloping womb of the earth – around the pole. By the time they were done, the Maypole was nearly invisible beneath a sheath of ribbons. If you have a large group of friends and lots of ribbon, you can easily hold your own Maypole Dance as part of your *Beltaine* festivities.

In some regions, however, a different maypole tradition existed: the carrying of highly decorated sticks with hoops or cross-sticks, or swags attached, covered with flowers, greenery or artificial materials such as crêpe paper. This tradition is known as garlanding, and was a central feature of May Day celebrations in central and southern England until the mid-19th century and is a more practical adaptation that we can use within our Craft celebrations as a lead-up to *Old Beltaine*. It can even be hung on the front door where the *Yule* wreath will later mark the Mid-Winter Festival.

The *Beltaine/Oestra* Bash

The *Beltaine* bonfire festival is really incomplete without a meal to go with it. For this occasion celebrate with foods that honour the earth but probably the most wide-spread tradition is that of 'Scottish Bannocks'. It is a form of flat bread, the same thickness as a scone cooked on a griddle or fried in a pan. Today it may also be baked in the oven for about twenty minutes. In parts of Scotland, the *Beltaine* bannock is a popular custom. It's said that if you eat one on *Beltaine* morning, you'll be guaranteed abundance for your crops and livestock.

Bannocks Or Oatcakes (Traditional)

Ingredients:

4 oz (⅔ cup) medium oatmeal
2 teaspoons melted fat (bacon dripping is good)

Pinch of bicarbonate of soda
Additional oatmeal for the kneading
Pinch of salt
¼ cup hot water

Process:

Mix the oatmeal with the salt and bicarbonate of soda in a basin, then make a well in the middle and pour in the melted fat. Stir around, then add enough water to make a stiff paste. Scatter a board or table thickly with oatmeal, turn out the mixture and roll into a ball. Knead well with the hands covered in oatmeal to prevent sticking. Press down a little and keep the edges as regular as possible. Then roll out to a ¼ inch thickness, and shape by putting a dinner plate on top and cutting round the edges. Sprinkle finally with a little meal, then cut into quarters or less. Place on the warmed girdle, or pan, and cook until the edges curl slightly. In Scotland they were finished on a toasting stone, but a medium hot grill to crisp the other side is adequate. [*A Taste of Scotland*]

Oatcakes are very good with fish, especially herrings, either smoked or fresh, with raw onions; also served with soups, butter-milk, or with jam, honey or marmalade for breakfast. Bannock is also a main staple of many indigenous communities in Canada because it's a simple bread that can be cooked in a pan, in the oven or over a fire. Top with butter, nut butter, jam or even melt a cube of cheese inside the dough. During *Beltaine* a bonfire is kept going all night long. Pieces of bannock are thrown into the fire as an offering.

Froissart, the 14th-century chronicler, writes that the Scottish soldier always carried a flat plate of metal and a wallet of oatmeal, as part of his equipment. With a little water he could always make himself an oatcake over a wood fire, which contributed to his remarkable stamina.

Loaded with beef, potatoes, and lots of vegetables, this dish celebrates winter and welcomes spring. It's warm and hearty, yet fresh and bright. And, at this time of year, when the days can fluctuate between spring-like with clear skies and warm air to cold and chilly rainy days that feel more like February, there's still justification to slow cook something cozy and savory for *Beltaine*. With the shifting weather, we never know if there's a last chilly day around the corner and this slow cooker beef stew has the best of both seasons. With tender beef cooked low and slow in a rich gravy along with spring veggies and plenty of fresh herbs, it's a set-it-and-forget-it recipe that simmers all day in your slow cooker.

Spring Beef And Vegetable Stew

Ingredients:

> 1 tbsp vegetable oil
> 500g beef diced stewing steak
> 1 tbsp flour
> 700ml beef stock
> 1 carrot, thickly sliced
> 400g Jersey Royal potatoes, cut into wedges
> 1 leek, thickly sliced
> 100g Spring Greens (or Baby Leaf Greens), shredded
> 25g pack fresh parsley, chopped
> Pepper and salt

Process:

Preheat the oven to 180ºC, gas mark 4. Heat the oil in a large frying pan and fry the beef until browned. Stir in the flour and seasoning and cook for 1 minute, add the stock and bring to the boil. Stir in the carrot and potatoes. Transfer to an ovenproof casserole dish (or slow cooker), cover and bake for 1 hour. Add the leek and bake for a further 1 hour until the beef is tender Add the greens and cook for 10 minutes. Stir in the parsley and serve with plenty of crusty bread [Waitrose]

Beltaine festivals, both in ancient times and today, are commonly accompanied by a large feast. Traditional *Beltaine* celebrations would set aside some food and drink for the *aos sí* as a nod of respect. Since *Beltaine* used to focus on livestock, perhaps it's not a bad alternative in providing an enormous 'cheese/ charcuterie board' with a wide variety of cheeses and cured meats for the occasion, together with a large wicker basket full of fresh bread and crackers. And best of all, this has something for everyone! From different types of cheese to sweet and savory snacks to crackers and cured meats, the best cheese boards leave no one behind.

Select the cheeses. Try to include a variety of flavors and textures by selecting cheeses from different families (for example):

- Aged: Aged Cheddar, Gruyere, Gouda.
- Soft: Brie, Camembert, Goat.
- Firm: Manchego, Parmigiano-Reggiano, Edam.
- Blue: Gorgonzola, Roquefort, Stilton.

Use cheese markers to label cheese so everyone knows what they're getting and bring cheeses to room temperature before serving in order to bring out their true flavor.

- **Add some charcuterie...** aka cured meats. Prosciutto, salami, sopressata, chorizo, mortadella or paté are all good options.

- **Add some savory...** Think olives, pickles, roasted peppers, artichokes or spicy mustards.
- **Add some sweet...** Think seasonal and dried fruits, candied nuts, preserves, honey or chutney.
- **Offer a variety of breads...** Sliced baguette, bread sticks, and a variety of crackers in different shapes, sizes, and flavors.
- **Finish it off with some garnishes...** This is a great way to give your cheese board a seasonal touch. Use edible flowers, cherry tomatoes, fresh herbs, celery or grapes to give your board the look and feel you want. [Lemon Tree Dwelling]

May Day Celebrations

The earliest known May celebrations appeared with the *Floralia*, festival of Flora, the Roman goddess of flowers, held from 27th April – 3rd May during the Roman Republic era, and the *Maiouma* or *Maiuma*, a festival celebrating Dionysus and Aphrodite held every three years during the month of May. The *Floralia* opened with theatrical performances. In which Ovid says that hares and goats were released as part of the festivities. Persius writes that crowds were pelted with vetches, beans, and lupins. A ritual called the *Florifertum* was performed on either 27th April or 3rd May, during which a bundle of wheat ears was carried into a shrine, though it is not clear if this devotion was made to Flora or Ceres. *Floralia* concluded with competitive events and spectacles, and a sacrifice to Flora.

It is an ancient festival marking the first day of summer, and a current traditional spring holiday in many European cultures. Dances, singing, and cake making are usually part of the festivities. In the late 20th century, many neo-pagans began reconstructing some of the older pagan festivals and combining them with more recently developed European secular and Catholic traditions, and celebrating May Day as a pagan religious festival. All spring fruits were eaten during the May Day meal. Crullers – a deep-fried pastry similar to a funnel cake – served with a fermented drink called sima, which is made with lemon juice, sugar, brown sugar, yeast and raisins were traditional foods served on May Day.

May Day Crullers – Tippaleivat

Ingredients:

2 eggs
1½ teaspoons sugar
½ teaspoon salt
2 cups flour
Vegetable oil for deep-fat frying
Confectioner's sugar
2 tablespoons lukewarm water
½ package (¾ teaspoon) of active dry or ½ cake of compressed yeast
1 cup milk, heated to lukewarm

Process:

Put the 2 tablespoons of lukewarm water into a small bowl and sprinkle in the yeast. Let it stand 2 or 3 minutes, then stir until the yeast is dissolved. Set the bowl in a warm, draft-free place (such as an unlighted oven) for 3 to 5 minutes, or until the yeast bubbles and the mixture doubles. Now stir in the lukewarm milk. n a large bowl, stir the eggs and sugar only long enough to combine them. Pour in the yeast mixture and, stirring briskly with a spoon, add the salt. Beat in the flour, ½ cup at a time, beating vigorously until a soft batter is formed. Cover with a kitchen towel and set in a warm place (again, the unlighted oven) for 1 hour, or until the batter has doubled in bulk, but do not let it stand longer. Pour enough oil into a deep-fat fryer or heavy 10- to 12-inch skillet to reach a depth of about 2 inches, and place over medium-high heat until the oil is very hot and a light haze forms above it. Spoon 1 cup of the batter into a pastry bag fitted with a ¼-inch plain tip. Holding the bag upright, squeeze the batter into the hot fat in a 3- to 4-inch circle, moving the bag in a circle to build a 'bird's nest' of 2 or 3 rings more or less atop one another. Deep-fry 2 or 3 crullers at a time, turning them over with a spatula or tongs after 1 minute, or when they are a golden brown. Fry the other side, then remove from the fat with a slotted spoon and drain on paper towels. When the crullers are cool, sift the sugar over them and serve with coffee or sima. [alleasyrecipies.com]

May Day, in both medieval and modern Europe, is a holiday for the celebration of the return of spring. The observance probably originated in ancient agricultural rituals, although later practices varied widely, the celebrations came to include the gathering of wildflowers and green branches, the weaving of floral garlands, the crowning of a May king and queen, and the setting up of a decorated May tree, or Maypole, around which people danced. Such rites originally may have been intended to ensure fertility for crops and, by extension, for livestock and humans, but in most cases this significance was gradually lost, so that the practices survived largely as popular festivities.

Among the many superstitions associated with May Day was the belief that washing the face with dew on the morning of 1st May would beautify the skin. Because the Puritans of New England considered the celebrations of May Day to be licentious and pagan, they forbade its observance, and the holiday never became an important part of American culture. In the 20th century, traditional May Day celebrations declined in many countries as May Day became associated with the international holiday honouring workers and the labour movement.

France: On 1 May 1561, King Charles IX of France received a lily of the valley as a lucky charm and he decided to offer a lily of the valley each year to the ladies of the court. At the beginning of the 20th century, it became custom to give a sprig of lily of the valley, a symbol of springtime, on May Day. The government permits individuals and workers' organisations to sell them tax-free on that single day. Nowadays, people may present loved ones either with bunches of lily of the valley or dog rose flowers.

In rural regions of **Germany**, especially the Harz Mountains, *Walpurgisnacht* celebrations of pagan origin are traditionally held on the night before May Day, including bonfires and the wrapping of a *Maibaum* (maypole). Young people use this opportunity to party, while the day itself is used by many families to get some fresh air. In the Rhineland, 1st May is also celebrated by the delivery of a maypole, a tree covered in streamers to the house of a girl the night before. The tree is typically from a love interest, though a tree wrapped only in white streamers is a sign of dislike. Women usually place roses or rice in the form of a heart at the house of their beloved one. It is common to stick the heart to a window or place it in front of the doormat. In leap years, it is the responsibility of the women to place the maypole. All the action is usually done secretly and it is an individual's choice whether to give a hint of their identity or stay anonymous. May Day was not established as a public holiday until the Third Reich declared 1st May a "national workers' day" in 1933.

Greece: Maios (Latin Maius), the month of May, took its name from the goddess Maia (Gr Μαία, the nurse), a Greek and Roman deity of fertility. The day of Maios celebrates the final victory of the summer against winter as the victory of life against death. The celebration is similar to an ancient ritual associated with another minor demi-god Adonis which also celebrated the revival of nature. There is today some conflation with yet another tradition, the revival or marriage of Dionysus (the god of theatre and wine-making). This event, however, was celebrated in ancient times not in May but in association with the *Anthesteria*, a festival held in February and dedicated to the goddess of agriculture Demeter and her daughter Persephone. Persephone emerged every year at the end of winter from the Underworld. The *Anthesteria* was a festival of souls, plants and flowers, and Persephone's return to the earth from Hades marked the rebirth of nature, a common theme in all these traditions.

What remains of the customs today, echoes these traditions of antiquity. A common, until recently, May Day custom involved the annual revival of a youth called Adonis, or alternatively of Dionysus, or of Maios. In a simple theatrical ritual, the significance of which has long been forgotten, a chorus of young girls sang a song over a youth lying on the ground, representing Adonis, Dionysus or Maios. At the end of the song, the youth rose up and a flower wreath was placed on his head.

The most common aspect of modern May Day celebrations is the preparation of a flower wreath from wild flowers, although as a result of urbanisation there is an increasing trend to buy wreaths from flower shops. The flowers are placed on the wreath against a background of green leaves and the wreath is hung either on the entrance to the family house/apartment or on a balcony. It remains there until midsummer night. On that night, the flower wreaths are set alight in bonfires known as Saint John's fires. Youths leap over the flames consuming the flower wreaths. This custom has also practically disappeared, like the theatrical revival of Adonis/Dionysus/Maios, as a result of rising urban traffic and with no alternative public grounds in most Greek city neighbourhoods.

In **Italy** it is called *Calendimaggio* or *cantar maggio* a seasonal feast held to celebrate the arrival of spring. The event takes its name from the period in which it takes place, that is, the beginning of May, from the Latin *calenda maia*. The *Calendimaggio* is a tradition still alive today in many regions of Italy as an allegory of the return to life and rebirth. This magical-propitiatory ritual is often performed during an almsgiving in which, in exchange for gifts (traditionally eggs, wine, food or sweets), the *Maggi* (or *maggerini*) sing auspicious verses to the inhabitants of the houses they visit. Throughout the Italian peninsula these *Il Maggio* couplets are very diverse – most are love songs with a strong romantic theme, that young people sang to celebrate the arrival of spring. Symbols of spring revival are the trees (alder, golden rain) and flowers (violets, roses), mentioned in the verses of the songs, and with which the *maggerini* adorn themselves. In particular the alder, which grows along the rivers, and is considered the symbol of life and that's why it is often present in the ritual.

Calendimaggio can be historically noted in Tuscany as a mythical character who had a predominant role and met many of the attributes of the god Belenus. In Lucania, the 'Maggi' have a clear auspicious character of pagan origin. In Syracuse, Sicily, the *Albero della Cuccagna* (cf. 'Greasy pole') is held during the month of May, a feast celebrated to commemorate the victory over the Athenians led by Nicias. However, Angelo de Gubernatis, in his work *Mythology of Plants*, believes that without doubt the festival preceded to that of said victory. It is a celebration that dates back to ancient peoples, and is very integrated with the rhythms of nature, such as the Celts (celebrating *Beltaine*), Etruscans and Ligures, in which the arrival of summer was of great importance.

'Maias' is a superstition throughout **Portugal**, with special focus on the northern territories and rarely elsewhere. Maias is the dominant naming in Northern Portugal, but it may be referred to by other names, including *Dia das Bruxas* (Witches' Day), *O Burro* (the Donkey, referring to an evil spirit) or the last of April, as the local traditions preserved to this day occur on that evening only. People put the yellow flowers of broom, the bushes are known as *giestas*. The flowers of the bush are known as Maias, which are placed on doors or gates and every doorway of houses, windows, granaries, currently also cars, which the populace collect on the evening of 30th April when the Portuguese brooms are blooming, to defend those places from bad spirits, witches and the evil eye. The placement of the flower or bush in the doorway must be done before midnight.

These festivities are a continuum of the 'Os Maios' of Galiza. In ancient times, this was done while playing traditional night-music. In some places, children were dressed in these flowers and went from place-to-place begging for money or bread. On 1st May, people also used to sing *Cantigas de Maio*, traditional songs related to this day and the whole month of May.

Romania: On May Day, the Romanians celebrate the *arminden* (or *armindeni*), the beginning of summer, symbolically tied with the protection of crops and farm animals. The name comes from Slavonic *Jeremiinŭ dĭnĭ*, meaning prophet Jeremiah's day, but the celebration rites and habits of this day are apotropaic and pagan (possibly originating in the cult of the god Pan).

The day is also called *ziua pelinului* ('mugwort day') or *ziua bețivilor* ('drunkards' day') and it is celebrated to ensure good wine in autumn and, for people and farm animals alike, good health and protection from the elements of nature (storms, hail, illness, pests). People would have parties in natural surroundings, with *lăutari* (fiddlers) for those who could afford it. Then it is customary to roast and eat lamb, along with new mutton cheese, and to drink mugwort-flavoured wine, or just red wine, to refresh the blood and get protection from diseases.

On the way back, the men wear lilac or mugwort flowers on their hats.

Other apotropaic rites include, in some areas of the country, people washing their faces with the morning dew (for good health) and adorning the gates for good luck and abundance with green branches or with birch saplings (for the houses with maiden girls). The entries to the animals' shelters are also adorned with green branches. All branches are left in place until the wheat harvest when they are used in the fire which will bake the first bread from the new wheat.

On May Day eve, country women do not work in the field as well as in the house to avoid devastating storms and hail coming down on the village. *Arminden* is also *ziua boilor* (oxen day) and thus the animals are not to be used for work, or else they could die or their owners could get ill. It is said that the weather is always good on May Day to allow people to celebrate.

There are so many festivals connected to the beginning of May as a start to summer that we're spoiled for choice to find ideas to implement into our own family observances. Family traditions are experiences or activities that are passed down between generations. These traditions can be as unique and special as the family itself. In addition to being something to look forward to, traditions also establish a foundation for family values and serve as special bonding experiences.

Chapter Five

An On-going Celebration

Living a pagan life-style is more than celebrating the eight important fire festivals each year and calling ourselves a witch. It's about observing the continuous calendar of events that may, or not, coincide with the civil calendar. Our seasonal festivals begin with this **Breath of Spring** ... to mark *Imbolc*/Candlemas on the 2nd February – which in turn marks the official end of the Yule celebrations and a traditional date by when all Yuletide decorations should be removed. Traditional witch, Evan John Jones, acknowledged that Candlemas is the first of the great Sabbats and the start of the ritual year, when it is time to let go of the past and to look to the future, clearing out the old, making both outer and inner space for new beginnings. Followed by the Spring or Vernal Equinox, Ostara and *Beltaine* to cover the months of spring before we prepare for the summer season ...

Sumer is Icumen In coincides with the ancient start of the traditional summer when our Ancestors turned the cattle out onto the summer pastures around the beginning of May, while the Summer Solstice marked the mid-summer in the Northern Hemisphere. Even though it's only June, we're already beginning the shift inward again. The days will continue to grow shorter until the harvest – when the sun is preparing to be reborn and we begin the cycle of growth all over again.

Harvest Home: In-Gathering is possibly the most sacred time of the witches' year that begins each year at Lammas as crops begin to ripen and the dark tide starts to turn. Lammas, also known as *Lughnasad*, is a pagan holiday and also one of the eight Wiccan sabbats during the year. Each marking a seasonal turning point.

Lammas occurs on 1st August, which is about halfway between the Summer Solstice and the Autumnal Equinox. During the Autumnal Equinox, the sun shines directly on the equator, and the northern and southern hemispheres get the same amount of rays.

Michaelmas was often used in the extended sense of autumn, as the name of the first term of the academic year, which begins at this time, at various educational institutions in the United Kingdom. Because it falls near the equinox, this holy day is also associated in the northern hemisphere with the beginning of autumn and the shortening of days. In medieval England, Michaelmas marked the ending and beginning of the husbandman's year when 'at that time harvest was over, and the hiring fairs would held at the end of September or beginning of October

Have A Cool Yule reminds us that Yuletide celebrations traditionally began at Samhain/ Halloween with the choosing of the 'Lord of Misrule' – while *the* Mid-Winter Festival at the Winter Solstice was the last feast celebration, before deep winter began. In 567CE the Council of Tours proclaimed that the entire period between Christmas and Epiphany should be considered part of the celebration, creating what became known as the 'Twelve Days of Christmas', or what the English called Christmastide. On the last of the twelve days, i.e. Twelfth Night, various cultures developed a wide range of additional special festivities. In some places, particularly South West England, Old Twelfth Night is still celebrated on 17th January. This continues the custom of the Apple Wassail on the date that corresponded to 6th January on the Julian calendar at the time of the change in calendars enacted by the Calendar Act of 1750. ...including the pagan cycle through until Candlemas when the Yuletide decorations were removed and the seasonal rites began all over again.

Many families have seasonal traditions that may have endured for generations. These special activities or events often generate fond memories that everyone cherishes and attempts to carry on into the future. Some traditions relate to the family's heritage, like going to a cultural festival, or cooking a meal from the 'old country' on a certain day each year. Still others are simply fun activities that family members enjoy repeating without any religious overlay. Establishing and maintaining family traditions is a way for extended families to bond over shared experiences – a way for them to connect to one another and to their past. But keeping family traditions going takes some commitment and planning. While most of us look forward to the stability and predictability that comes with repeating the same activities each year, it also can be daunting if the family traditions are highly involved, overly expensive, or require a lot of planning.

When creating our own family traditions, we should try to keep them simple. Think about playing games, sharing special recipes, going on a hike, watching a performance, and so on. These simpler traditions are more likely to be repeated and carried on. Likewise, our traditions do not need to cost a lot of money. There are plenty of ways for families to bond without spending money and traditions can provide families with a strong sense of identity and belonging. They can inspire positive feelings and memories that family members can share. Family traditions also provide a sense of continuity across generations. They are a way of transferring the family's values, history, and culture from one generation to the next under the umbrella of modern or neo-paganism.

Nevertheless, modern paganism generally encompasses any of several spiritual elements that attempt to revive the ancient polytheistic religions of Europe and the Middle East. These movements have a close relationship to ritual magic and modern witchcraft. Neo-Paganism differs from them, however, in striving to revive authentic pantheons and rituals of ancient cultures, though often in deliberately eclectic and reconstructionist ways, and by a particularly contemplative and celebrative attitude. Typically people with romantic feelings toward nature and deep ecological concerns, Neo-Pagans centre their dramatic and colourful rituals around the changes of the seasons and the personification of nature as full of divine life, as well as the holy days and motifs of the religions by which their own groups are inspired. [Britannica]

Paganism's public rituals are generally seasonal, although the pre-Christian festivals that we use as a basis vary across Europe. Nevertheless, common to almost all pagan beliefs is an emphasis on an agrarian cycle and respect for the Ancestors. Popular public festivals include those marking the Summer and Winter Solstices as well as the Equinoxes at the start of spring and the harvest. On a more formal basis our traditional Old Craft beliefs can be seen as a form of Ancestor-worship that focus on *Samhain*/Halloween – the beginning of the Yuletide celebrations in olden times and the start of winter.

There is an increasing awareness in the academic world that paganism *does* have something to say, and that it plays a role in the gradual interconnectedness of spiritualities within the UK; although they share similarities, contemporary pagan movements are diverse, and do not share a single set of beliefs, practices, or texts. Which leads to many pagans of a more traditional nature choosing to keep their beliefs private to avoid discrimination and ostracism even in today's so-called liberal climate. Don't forget that those who were at the coal-face of prejudice during the 1960s ... 70s ... 80s ... are *today's* grandparents!

People create and maintain family traditions because they bring meaning to celebrations and foster special bonds in *today's* children. Children love routine and consistency; a family tradition provides this year after year. It also helps the children manage the changes in the year and gives them something to look forward to. In addition, family traditions enhance family and personal well-being and can also strengthen the family identity. More importantly, traditions create positive experiences and memories for everyone by nurturing a family's connection and giving them a sense of belonging that has been passed down from one generation to the next. And yet, there are those pagans who claim that these established traditions are elitist and out-dated!

According to various parenting and family organizations, by their very nature, traditions are *supposed* to evolve constantly and meet the changing requirements of time and social contexts but it's ridiculous how some tend to use the word 'tradition' when connected with neo-paganism as being synonymous with retrogressive and anti-freedom. They want us to treat our tradition as a liability and not as an asset so that we become mindless apes of the neo-pagan lifestyle. Fortunately, most traditionalists know that their customs, if handled judiciously, can be great assets for pagan society et al. They connect our past with our present and the future. People without roots in the past cannot have a creative sense of the here and now.

Sometimes it can seem like the whole world changes overnight, every night. Divorce, a change of faith, blended families, single parents and tragedy can make us feel like the family units that many of us came from are a thing of the past. Often, our family traditions seem like the only things keeping us together, linking our past generations with the bright hopes of our future. In truth, almost every family tradition has its roots in necessity. Over time, that necessity becomes nostalgia, and eventually, it just becomes another way for families to relate and connect with one another. As families evolve and change, those traditions once again become necessities, as they assume new meaning in the context of our need to communicate and understand our loved ones.

A family dinner, for example – whether nightly, weekly or just on holidays – often carries with it a lot of small but beautifully significant memories, associations and kindnesses. While our concept of family dinner may descend from a prior generation's beginnings in this country, let's say, it's those same traditions that we choose to preserve that keep us from sitting at the table, many years later, playing on our phones and ignoring each other. With packed schedules for both kids and parents these days, it's all too easy for family dinner to go on the backburner. And though a seated family dinner can't happen every single night – we're only human after all! – research suggests that sharing dinner together should be a top priority for all families. From increased academic performance to higher self-esteem, kids tend to be happier and healthier when they experience regular family meals. [ACTIVEkids]

A great deal of the reason behind the usual traditional holidays and observances, in fact, is about establishing a healthy and meaningful purpose for coming together. The summer and/ or Easter holidays only come once a year, and even for the most secular family, they provide the simple pleasure of knowing that we'll see our loved ones at least that often. For more religiously observant families, the holidays still provide a healthy reminder to let the world go on spinning while we connect with our families and engage in our heritage together. Many of our traditions make a lot more sense if we look at them that way: not the holiday itself, but the pretext it gives us to affirm our faith – not just in our beliefs or our cultural duties, but our faith in our families and the love we share, too.

For many of us, finding a balance of traditions can become a nightmare. A blended family, one with step-parents, can end up heading into nuclear meltdown over something as simple as when Christmas gifts should be opened. This is because we base a lot of our emotional and family lives in traditions, even those we might normally say aren't very important. Because our traditions only occur at specific times, or under specific circumstances, we often make emotional connections during those times that only flare up once they've reawakened. Feelings that were hurt as children can re-surface, old wounds and resentments can reopen, and lost or absent family members' presence is more sorely missed. Which is why this series of books is each sub-titled: 'How to Survive (and Enjoy) the various Seasonal Holidays'!

Likewise, positive feelings and situations are often relegated to traditional times and holidays that we spend together and it's possible that as children age and scatter, the holidays are the only time the whole family is together. That's not a sad thing, but a joyful one and it's encoded in each tiny tradition that we each share over those times, from the traditional dishes we make and serve together – to the jokes that nobody seems to remember the rest of the year. A family is a moving target: not just Mom and Pop and two-and-a-half kids, but who those kids became, their mates and children, and all the traditions they've imported as a result. But our family is also forever: the only group that we're born connected to – and remain connected to – for our whole life. When we look at it this way, we can see that what we call 'family' is really just one frame in a long, long movie. [HowStuffWorks]

Tradition ties us all upward into our family trees, and down into the families that are still being created. It's a way of honoring our Ancestors and departed family members, and of welcoming new members in. Family traditions are *physical* representations of our place in a never-ending saga that includes everyone we've ever loved, and everybody they've ever loved, and so on. Observing and preserving tradition, and teaching it to our children, grounds us all in an ongoing project that will last far beyond our own short time on Earth.

Needless to say, it's a good idea to allow some holiday traditions to grow and change, just like our family does. As the saying goes, it's important to give ourselves and our children both roots and wings. What that means, of course, is that – as families and individuals – we allow ourselves to grow and change, to accept differences and adjust traditions as the time comes. For some, that can be desperately hard to do, but it's essential. Holding onto traditions strictly for their own sake, however, does nobody any favors. Every holiday is an opportunity to examine our own traditions and their meaning to our family as it stands today. By changing a single aspect of the holiday – to accommodate far-flung family members, for example – have we really destroyed the holiday itself? Or have we allowed flexibility to bring the family closer together in the spirit of that tradition?

Holidays and traditional gatherings are notorious for power plays and old resentments. If we find ourselves or a family member stressing about changing a tradition, it's important to be honest with ourselves *and* them about what that tradition means to you both, and what parts of that tradition carry the most meaning. We're always told that etiquette and manners make people feel more comfortable, never less comfortable. Like the finer points of etiquette, when an old family tradition causes more trouble than it brings joy, it may be time to let it go. We cannot be slaves to traditions any more than we should simply let them slide. The point is to keep our families warm and strong, both in our memories and in the comfort they bring us, during the rest of the year. Anything less just isn't worth the ruffled feathers.

Because there is no formal liturgy to connect those of a pagan persuasion from different generations, there is generally no problem in arranging a traditional celebration that can include friends and family who do not share our beliefs, because we are not holding any formal rites or rituals that they may find confusing or offensive. It also goes without saying that a party-political broadcast on behalf of the pagan party – or a full-scale bells and smells seasonal ritual – should not part of the entertainment. Over the years, most pagans of my acquaintance have become pretty adept at throwing seasonal parties and integrating 'cowans' (i.e. non-witches) into the mix without too much trouble.

In my experience, however, the greatest party-poopers are those *fringe*-believers who insist on regaling any listener(s) to their idiot's guide to *Beltaine* speech that they've gleaned from their monthly subscription to a mind, body and spirit magazine. We have one in our 'circle' of acquaintances, who is completely unaware that their hosts are the Dame and Magister of a very prestigious coven but, not being a couple to promote themselves, the erstwhile 'expert' is sadly ignorant of their standing in the pagan community – much to the amusement of those in the *know*. Especially when the guest announced loudly that she'd been appointed 'creatrix' to a local pagan group because of her wide-reaching knowledge and, because the group leader was impressed by her grasp of contemporary witchcraft!

A Creatrix is a woman who is deeply connected to herself as a Woman and the Feminine Source of Creative power. She gives rise to desires, gives birth to ideas and life of all kinds. She dreams courageously and trusts so deeply in the intrinsic co-creative connection she shares with the Divine and the Natural World. She nurtures herself, those around her and the planet. She is the guardian and protector of the magical essence of life. She understands that without darkness there is no light. Without the beautiful presence of the masculine in our world there is no wholeness. To be a Master Creatrix she accepts the power of owning her shadow side and being vulnerable is **the s**uperpower of living *freely, fully and creatively.* [GoddessFlow]

This kind of jargon is 'the technical terminology or characteristic idiom of a special activity or group', and may not be properly understood outside that context ... Instead, here we had a person who simply doesn't know the right words but who was just trying to use jargon to feel important ... but it kept the Magister amused for hours! Try to avoid this kind of guest to avoid embarrassment or unpleasantness.

In these books, we are reminded how to enjoy *and* survive the various seasonal celebrations that were traditionally part and parcel of our ancestral beliefs before they were assimilated into the church calendar. Here we are encouraged to claim back our own customs and traditions by re-establishing seasonal recipes and the common way of doing things; something that many people did, and have done for a long time – usually, those people coming from the same country, region, culture, or belief. So, if for example, our Polish grandmother tells us about the traditional celebrations remembered from her childhood, now might be a good time to listen ... before grandma is gone and the memories forgotten.

Bibliography & Sources

Taking a leaf out of Aleister Crowley's book, it is always a good move to go from each respected author to those that have been quoted in the text or bibliography:

> It established a rational consecution in my research; and as soon as I reached a certain point the curves became re-entrant, so that my knowledge acquired a comprehensiveness which could never have been so satisfactorily attained by any arbitrary curriculum. I began to understand the real relation of one subject to another ...

This technique often takes us to valuable out-of-print volumes that contain material not to be found repeated *ad nauseam* on the internet and this in turn, gives our own reading and writing a sense of newness and fresh insight.

The Four Seasons: The Living Countryside (Reader's Digest)
The (Inner-City) Path, Melusine Draco (Moon Books)
Round About the Cauldron Go ..., Phillip Wright and Carrie West (ignotus)
Seasonal Feasts & Festivals, E O James (Thames & Hudson)
A Taste of Scotland, Theodora Fitzgibbon (Pan)

MOON
BOOKS

PAGANISM & SHAMANISM

What is Paganism? A religion, a spirituality, an alternative belief system, nature worship? You can find support for all these definitions (and many more) in dictionaries, encyclopaedias, and text books of religion, but subscribe to any one and the truth will evade you. Above all Paganism is a creative pursuit, an encounter with reality, an exploration of meaning and an expression of the soul. Druids, Heathens, Wiccans and others, all contribute their insights and literary riches to the Pagan tradition. Moon Books invites you to begin or to deepen your own encounter, right here, right now.

If you have enjoyed this book, why not tell other readers by posting a review on your preferred book site.

Recent bestsellers from Moon Books are:

Journey to the Dark Goddess
How to Return to Your Soul
Jane Meredith
Discover the powerful secrets of the Dark Goddess and
transform your depression, grief and pain into healing
and integration.
Paperback: 978-1-84694-677-6 ebook: 978-1-78099-223-5

Shamanic Reiki
Expanded Ways of Working with Universal Life Force Energy
Llyn Roberts, Robert Levy
Shamanism and Reiki are each powerful ways of healing; together,
their power multiplies. *Shamanic Reiki* introduces techniques to
help healers and Reiki practitioners tap ancient healing wisdom.
Paperback: 978-1-84694-037-8 ebook: 978-1-84694-650-9

Pagan Portals – The Awen Alone
Walking the Path of the Solitary Druid
Joanna van der Hoeven
An introductory guide for the solitary Druid, *The Awen Alone* will
accompany you as you explore, and seek out your own place
within the natural world.
Paperback: 978-1-78279-547-6 ebook: 978-1-78279-546-9

A Kitchen Witch's World of Magical Herbs & Plants
Rachel Patterson
A journey into the magical world of herbs and plants, filled with
magical uses, folklore, history and practical magic. By popular
writer, blogger and kitchen witch, Tansy Firedragon.
Paperback: 978-1-78279-621-3 ebook: 978-1-78279-620-6

Medicine for the Soul
The Complete Book of Shamanic Healing
Ross Heaven
All you will ever need to know about shamanic healing and how to
become your own shaman...
Paperback: 978-1-78099-419-2 ebook: 978-1-78099-420-8

Shaman Pathways – The Druid Shaman
Exploring the Celtic Otherworld
Danu Forest
A practical guide to Celtic shamanism with exercises and
techniques as well as traditional lore for exploring the Celtic
Otherworld.
Paperback: 978-1-78099-615-8 ebook: 978-1-78099-616-5

Traditional Witchcraft for the Woods and Forests
A Witch's Guide to the Woodland with Guided Meditations and
Pathworking
Mélusine Draco
A Witch's guide to walking alone in the woods, with guided
meditations and pathworking.
Paperback: 978-1-84694-803-9 ebook: 978-1-84694-804-6

Wild Earth, Wild Soul
A Manual for an Ecstatic Culture
Bill Pfeiffer
Imagine a nature-based culture so alive and so connected,
spreading like wildfire. This book is the first flame...
Paperback: 978-1-78099-187-0 ebook: 978-1-78099-188-7

Naming the Goddess
Trevor Greenfield
Naming the Goddess is written by over eighty adherents and
scholars of Goddess and Goddess Spirituality.
Paperback: 978-1-78279-476-9 ebook: 978-1-78279-475-2

Shapeshifting into Higher Consciousness
Heal and Transform Yourself and Our World with Ancient
Shamanic and Modern Methods
Llyn Roberts
Ancient and modern methods that you can use every day to
transform yourself and make a positive difference in the world.
Paperback: 978-1-84694-843-5 ebook: 978-1-84694-844-2

Readers of ebooks can buy or view any of these bestsellers by
clicking on the live link in the title. Most titles are published in
paperback and as an ebook. Paperbacks are available in traditional
bookshops. Both print and ebook formats are available online.

Find more titles and sign up to our readers' newsletter at
http://www.johnhuntpublishing.com/paganism
Follow us on Facebook at https://www.facebook.com/MoonBooks
and Twitter at https://twitter.com/MoonBooksJHP